BACK HOME IN
WILLIAMSON
COUNTY

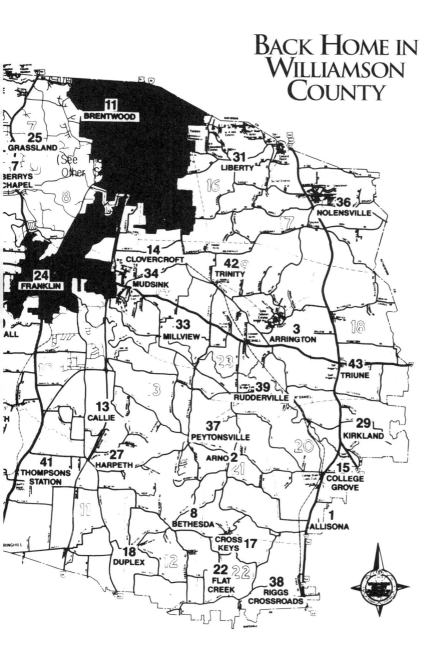

LYN SULLIVAN PEWITT

BACK HOME IN WILLIAMSON COUNTY

BICENTENNIAL
EDITION

HILLSBORO PRESS
Franklin, Tennessee

TENNESSEE HERITAGE LIBRARY
Bicentennial Collection

Text originally published as *Back Home in Williamson County: A Project of Homecoming '86,* © 1986 Lyn Sullivan Pewitt.

Printed in the United States of America

00   99   98   97   96   6   5   4   3   2   1

Library of Congress Cataloging-in-Publication Data

Pewitt, Lyn Sullivan.
    Back home in Williamson County / Lyn Sullivan Pewitt. — Bicentennial ed.
        p.   cm.
    Originally published: Franklin, Tenn. : Williamson County Bank, 1986.
    Includes bibliographical references and index.
    ISBN 1-881576-60-4
    1. Williamson County (Tenn.)—History. 2. Williamson County (Tenn.)—Pictorial works.   I. Title.
F443.W7P49   1996
976.8'56—dc20   95-47234
                                      CIP

All photography by Mayhew Koellein, except the photo used on p. 90, courtesy of Gilbert Sullivan. Cover photos by Mayhew Koellein.

Cover by Bozeman Design.

Bicentennial Edition update by Rick Warwick.

Although the author and publisher have carefully researched all sources to ensure the accuracy and completeness of the information contained in this book, we assume no responsibility for errors, inaccuracies, omissions or any inconsistency herein. Any slights of people or organizations are unintentional.

Published by
HILLSBORO PRESS
an imprint of
PROVIDENCE HOUSE PUBLISHERS
238 Seaboard Lane • Franklin, Tennessee 37067
800-321-5692

To Gale

From the Carnton Mansion to Big Foot Lane

Thank you for your patience and your
continuing love of Williamson County.

To the residents of Williamson County

May those who have come before help define
the generations of the future.

Contents

Foreword

WHEN LYN SULLIVAN WROTE *Back Home in Williamson County* during Tennessee's homecoming celebration in 1986, Williamson County was in the midst of enjoying one of its greatest periods of growth since being established in 1799. During the decade of the 1980s, the county's population jumped from fifty-eight thousand to eighty-one thousand, and today that figure hovers near the one hundred thousand mark. Only recently named by the *Wall Street Journal* as one of America's top twenty communities for business relocation, the region has been swamped the past few years with business and residential development.

When Lyn wrote her book, our county was in the final stages of deserting its rural roots and becoming a first-rate cosmopolitan region. With Tennessee's largest per capita income, we Williamson Countians thrive in affluency seldom experienced by counties that only twenty or so years ago were still predominantly agricultural in nature. Yet, we have managed to preserve many of our smaller neighborhoods and communities in much the same condition as they existed fifty years ago.

It is the lore and romance of these rural villages—Nolensville, College Grove, Burwood, Flat Creek, and many others—that Lyn Sullivan has captured in *Back Home in Williamson County*. These places—and the generations of rural folks who have lived there for the past two hundred years—are the backbone of our county's history, and while both the places and the people are being gobbled up at an alarming rate by so-called "progress," it is they to whom we must look if we are to obtain relief from today's high-tech world of computers, mind-boggling finances, corporate takeovers, and too-rapid community expansion.

Lyn Sullivan is to be commended for re-issuing *Back Home in Williamson County* at this very critical benchmark in our county's development. Perhaps, to those of us who remember the "good old days," it will refresh our memories of how things used to be in the days of our youth. And to those newer generations, it is sure to enlighten, entertain, and give valuable food for thought about the future choices each of us must make about our lifestyle, environment, and peace of mind.

—James A. Crutchfield
Executive Editor
Tennessee Heritage Library
Franklin, Tennessee

Preface and Acknowledgments

I T WAS A HOT JUNE DAY IN 1986 AT COLLEGE GROVE when *Back Home in Williamson County* made its debut. This was the first of many Homecoming '86 celebrations to take place in the county. On Saturdays I would load my supply of books, a card table draped with the Tennessee state flag, selected photos from the book displayed on a large stand-up folding screen (which always fell down even in the slightest breeze), and set up my stand under a tent or out in the summer sun to promote a book with vignettes about the people who helped shape the heritage of our county. I was able to meet once again with those who had assisted me with the histories and to make new friends of those who came to purchase or merely browse. One of my favorite comments came from a gentleman in the Flat Creek community who said: "I liked your book. After the Bible, it's the best book I've ever read." In the past ten years, I have received letters from all parts of the country from people who have an interest in learning more about their ancestors or those who wish to share some additional information with me.

This is a new version of the 1986 edition. Much of the information remains the same, but such well-respected historians as Richard Warwick and James Crutchfield have assisted with necessary corrections in the historical content and updating names of residents in some of the beautiful old homes that abound in the county.

I'm very proud to have *Back Home in Williamson County* as part of the Tennessee Heritage Library. Special thanks to Mary Bray Wheeler and also to Andrew B. Miller for encouraging me to reissue the book; to Jo Jaworski and Trinda Cole for making the updated version even better than the original; and to Mayhew Koellein who has always had an eye for seeing the unique and intriguing in our surroundings. His photographs make us aware of how much the area has changed.

Special thanks to Jim, Mike, Pat, and Kate for being themselves; and thanks also to a very welcoming Pewitt family including Sue Pewitt Lewis, Brad Pewitt, Bonnie Pewitt Derylo, and Dudley Pewitt Swiney.

I would be remiss if I didn't thank Jimmy and Marsha French, Tom Liddell, and Tom Lawrence, the ones who formulated the project back in 1983 when it was a means of promoting Williamson County Bank and a useful source for gathering information on the changing county. Thanks also to the owners of WAKM Radio: Jim Hayes, Charles Dibrell, Bill Ewin, and Darrell Williams, my employers at the time, for the opportunity to drive the backroads of the county and meet firsthand some of the gracious people who are keepers of our heritage.

I am especially grateful to Louise Lynch and Virginia Bowman who continue to keep up with the history of the county and who were so unselfish in sharing their many hours of work with me.

My hope is that this book will encourage natives and newcomers alike to learn more about the people and places who helped shape the Williamson County we know today.

1

Allisona

THE SMALL COMMUNITY OF ALLISONA, located in the southeast corner of the county, was listed on the county map of 1878 as Jordan's Store. Jordan's Store was built after 1841. When the government put a post office in the store, Johnson Jordan decided to name the village "Allisona" in honor of his wife, Margaret W. Allison. Before Jordan's Store was the name of the area, the village of Harpeth Lick, near the William Ogilvie pioneer home, sheltered early settlers. The Harpeth Lick Cumberland Presbyterian Church stands as a monument to this early village, named for the lick on the river where the deer came to get salt.

The community once had a flour mill run by a Mr. Swan. There were also several cotton gins, a blacksmith shop, a sawmill, and a tobacco factory. The tobacco factory previously housed one of the two stores in the community and was bought by James Wilhoite in 1873. The factory operated until 1908 when it was torn down by Cowden McCord Covington. There was also a cotton factory in Allisona, and according to an article in the *Western Weekly Review*, it was destroyed by a morning fire September 30, 1856.

The Allisona sawmill supplied cords of wood at one dollar a cord to fuel the steam engines, which ran from Nashville to Birmingham. The trains were used to haul livestock—cattle, hogs, and sheep—to the nearest market, which was Louisville, Kentucky. Local farmers were usually paid for their animals before they were shipped, getting the best price before the animals lost weight on their journey to market.

Two schools served the children of Allisona: the Simmons Hill School, a one-room schoolhouse which ran through the eighth grade, and the Harpeth Lick Grammar School. This school met in the Harpeth Lick Cumberland Presbyterian Church during the week.

The Allisona Church of Christ was started in 1941, when Monroe Lamb of Nashville came to the community and talked to Zelma White about holding a tent meeting near the site of the present church. He asked her husband Melvin White to go to Nashville and secure a tent for the meeting. Harry Fox held the meeting and five people were baptized. The church was officially started in an old storehouse and later moved to its present location on the Horton Highway. For the first few years, there were different preachers each Sunday, with Monroe Lamb conducting the majority of the services.

The Mount Zion Methodist Episcopal Church, near Allisona, was organized in 1869. The original church was located on a one-acre hillside near the present site on land donated by Laban Creswell. In November 1911, the original one-acre lot was exchanged for one of equal value nearby but on level ground. The present structure was built in 1912 and at one time, served as a school.

Several sources agree there was a Camp Harris at Allisona during the Civil War, but there are conflicting reports as to whether it was a Union or Confederate camp.

The first automobile came to Allisona in the early 1920s when Terry White purchased a 1921 Ford. He soon found himself besieged by friends and neighbors asking him to take them to the doctor in College Grove or shopping in Franklin. White's car was bought for about $600 and had a gas tank which only held five gallons of gas. The first truck in the area was also a Ford, had solid tires without inner tubes, and was used to haul livestock. Before the days of cars and trucks the young men of the community would groom and decorate their horses and then race them down the road, just like the teenagers today do with their cars.

The focal point of Allisona today is Rigsby's Store and Garage, which was started around 1930, replacing Brisby's Store. Rigsby's still occupies the same cinder block building on the corner of Allisona-Arno Road, but the mechanic shop, which had a dirt floor and was just behind the general store, was moved to one side of the structure and had a concrete floor added. Allisona still has several magnificent homes like the one formerly occupied by Della Covington Corlette and built along the Horton Highway in 1880.

Interior of Rigsby's Store. Left to right: J. W. Rigsby, Will Clarkson, Clarence Graham.

In the early years, people came from miles around to trade at Jordan's Store because of the fine quality merchandise he carried. Today it's a community where people enjoy coming back to greet old friends and neighbors, and many young people who leave for jobs in larger cities, often return to the peace and quiet of Allisona in their retirement years.

2

Arno

COOL SPRINGS PRIMITIVE CHURCH
DATES BACK TO 1818

THE COMMUNITY OF ARNO, unlike most communities and towns, is not named for early settlers, businesses, or a unique feature about the area. The government christened the community Arno when a post office was located there in the early 1900s. Before that, mail came from Franklin once a week.

One early settler was William Kennedy, born in Virginia in 1755. He served in the Revolutionary War and was taken prisoner in Virginia in 1781. Conditions were so deplorable in the prison that out of sixty men, only seven lived. Kennedy came to Williamson County in 1818, buying seventy-two acres of land on McCrory's Creek. He died in 1853 and is buried at Arno. Other early settlers include the Rucker family: William Rucker Sr., his son William Jr., another son John, and son's-in-law, William Hatcher and William Burns. Later families include the Demonbreun, Wilson, Lanier, Davis, and Adair families.

The Cool Springs Baptist Church dates back to 1818 and the Wesley Chapel United Methodist Church was built around 1834 on Owen Hill Road. The little community began to grow at the turn of the century with stores, schools, churches, a doctor, and even a veterinarian serving the area. Dr. Lowe was one of the first doctors in Arno, living about a mile from the Smithson's Store. Dr. W. W. Graham was the next physician, traveling the roads by horse and buggy day and night to care for his patients. C. R. Pennington was the county veterinarian and also its blacksmith. John G. Hall owned a tobacco factory at Arno before 1860.

The first store was built in 1893. E. K. Smithson owned and operated the business until 1925. From 1935 until 1946 it was run by Eugene "Red" Jordan and Earl Culberson. Gasoline sold for twenty cents a gallon and supplies were purchased twice a week in Nashville. Once a week they would take livestock to the old Union Stockyards in Nashville and return with produce from the C. B. Ragland Co. Another day, chickens and eggs would be shipped to market. In the summer months the truck would stop at the icehouse in Franklin for 300 pounds of ice. With this, the ladies of Arno would make homemade ice cream. The store was the scene of several memorable incidents. One day in February 1940, when the county had been experiencing several days of subfreezing cold, a woman shot a man about a mile and a half from the store. Gun in hand she trudged the distance to the store. When she walked into the building still holding the firearm, the men swapping tales around the potbellied stove scattered in a hurry. Red Jordan called the sheriff, Gilbert Sullivan, who removed her from the premises.

Electricity came to Arno in 1943, and one day C. R. Pennington, the blacksmith, stopped by the store to purchase light bulbs for his home. After he inserted the bulbs in the lamps, he returned them to the store, telling Red Jordan he hadn't realized his wife was such a terrible housekeeper.

Earl Culberson joined the army during World War II, returning home to take a job as the postmaster at College Grove, while Jordan left the store in 1946 to run a dairy farm. The store has known many owners over the years: Bob White, Jimmy Robinson, John Paul Skinner, Frank Howell, and Fred Hughes. Milton Ryan was the final owner before this piece of Williamson County history burned in October 1982.

The Cool Springs Primitive Baptist Church, started around 1818, is still going strong with 250 to 300 members making up the congregation. The original church was located near a springs and the name was kept when the church moved. In 1912, the minister died preaching a sermon from the pulpit, and the grandfather of the late Elder Milton Lillard, was a witness. During the Civil War, church records indicate services were called off on several occasions because of both Yankee and Confederate soldiers pillaging in the area. Each year the church has an annual meeting for which members and former members gather. According to the late Milton Lillard, many of the older folks met their mates at those June meetings.

There was also a Cool Springs School, and Phil Bennett, who lived to be over 100, was the last student from the school. The Arno School went through the eighth grade and the teacher was paid fifty dollars a month for her work. Children would collect kindling to make fires in the wood stove and the reward for their labors would be a wienie roast. Mr. and Mrs. J. H. Pylant were principal and teacher for many years. In the early thirties, Mrs. Pylant would take some of the children in her car to Franklin to participate in Blue Ribbon Day. This was the day the public health nurse examined all

Wesley Chapel Methodist Church was started in 1834 by the "Four Billys," William Hatcher, William Rucker, William Burns, and William Lanier. Land for the building was donated by Rucker on Owen Hill Road and the first church was built of home-made bricks. It was built near a spring so the congregation could have good drinking water. In 1835 the church was dedicated and used until 1907 when the building was torn down to make way for a new structure. This chapel was made of wood and built on Arno Road. Brick from the original building was sold and the original lumber put into the second building. Wesley Chapel became a part of the College Grove circuit, along with the church at College Grove and one at Triune. The current church was completed in 1962, on the same site, and built of brick.

the children in the communities, and if they were fine specimens of health, they were given blue ribbons. Each summer, one day was set aside for a Blue Ribbon Day parade, when the county school children marched down the streets of Franklin, proudly wearing their blue ribbons. Arno School, being one of the first alphabetically, led the parade. Some of the teachers at the Arno School included A. R. Parks, Tom Pettus, Miss Stella Parks, Sally Hudson, Miss Nimmie Cullum, T. R. Beasley, Miss Ellen Smithson, Miss Virginia Graves, Mildred Arnold, Josephine Cousin, Miss Mary Walton, and Miss Elmira Petway. Arno School was a vital part of the community until it closed in 1947.

The main thoroughfare through Arno was once a toll road. Red Jordan's father helped build the road so the family was allowed to drive it at no charge. One year, J. R. Rucker spent so much time working on the road, his crops suffered. There were tollgates by the Hatcher farm and the Epworth Methodist Church. Cost for going down the road through the gate was a nickel for a horse and rider, a dime for a buggy, and after midnight, the gate was left up. Travelers only had to pay going one way if they came back the same day. Every male over the age of twenty-one had to pay toll or work on the road, and during the summer, at least one week was set aside for road repairs which were done by the men of the community. The first auto in Arno was a Studebaker owned by E. K. Smithson.

During the 1940s, all the small communities had baseball teams and would face each other in Saturday afternoon contests. The rivalry between Arno and Bethesda was not unlike that of Vanderbilt and Tennessee.

Children in Arno were like those anywhere else; they liked to be mischievous. One man in the area liked to buy salted fish from the store. Before they were eaten, the fish had to be soaked overnight in the creek. One night some boys saw him put the fish in the creek and, just for fun, pull them out of the water so only the tails were in the creek. By the time he came back the next morning, the mischief makers had put the fish back in, so he was none the wiser, until his wife cooked them. He had some very salty fish for breakfast.

The Arno community is still made up of generous friends and neighbors, and while their gathering place, the store on Arno Road, no longer exists, good memories and good people are never far away. New people are moving into Arno, buying and building homes; new residents are joining the churches, and Arno is enjoying a rebirth like so much of Williamson County.

3

Arrington

ONCE KNOWN AS
PETERSBURG

T HE COMMUNITY OF ARRINGTON, now about ten miles east of Franklin, was once located on Nolensville Pike where the Arrington Church of Christ now stands. But the current Arrington wasn't even Arrington—it was called Petersburg. Because there was already a Petersburg in Bedford County, the name was changed to Arrington in 1858 when a post office was established. The name "Petersburg" was suggested by David Sayers in honor of Peter Walker, an early preacher in the area. "Arrington" came from the name of the creek which ran through the Paschall farm.

The Paschalls, one of the foremost families in the community, came to Arrington in 1830 when Edwin Paschall moved from Virginia to teach at Union Academy. Other early settlers include the Roberts, Crocketts, Sayers, Scales, and Edmondson families. Edwin Paschall was the father of Dr. B. H. Paschall, and great-grandfather of Hill Paschall, presently a realtor in Franklin. Dr. Benjamin Paschall was one of the early well-known physicians in the county, having a practice which extended from Nolensville to College Grove and into Franklin, which he covered by horseback and horse and buggy. Dr. B. H. Paschall was also Arrington's first postmaster, with the post office located in one corner of his doctor's office. The office was about 300 yards north of the intersection of Wilson Pike and Highway 96 East.

Early mail was brought to the post office three times a week from Brentwood by horseback, and in 1914, the Lewisburg & Northern Railway came through about a mile west of Arrington. At that time, the son of Dr. Paschall, Benjamin Hillyard Paschall, was postmaster. Looking at an old

8

Williamson County map, the word "Benhill" is a short distance from the word "Arrington." The name Arrington was too close to that of Arlington, Tennessee, or Texas, and in the 1940s the government asked the community to change the name at the depot only. They asked the postmaster if he would consider lending his name to the train depot. Benjamin Hillyard Paschall added the name "Benhill" to the community. The depot is long since gone, but the name is still on the map. Hill Paschall became postmaster of Arrington, replacing his father, and was in that position for thirty years. When he retired in 1971, it was the end of three generations of Paschalls serving as postmaster in the Arrington community.

Paschall's Store, located on Highway 96 East and Wilson Pike, was the most prominent landmark of the community. The original store was lost when the highway cut through the area, but Hill and Evelyn Paschall rebuilt the store at its present location in 1939. At one time, it was one of the two largest general stores in Tennessee, the other being Ogles Store in Gatlinburg. Along with groceries, they sold shoes, hardware, coal, seeds, building materials, and gasoline. The Arrington Post Office was in one corner of the store. Hill and Evelyn remember when gasoline was sixteen cents a gallon, domestic sold for seven cents a yard, and eggs, purchased for three cents a dozen, were taken to Nashville and sold for four cents a dozen. At its peak years of 1958 to 1963, there were as many as seventeen employees at the store. The Paschalls had drawings every Saturday night to give away groceries, fruit baskets, and during World War II, savings bonds.

Hill Paschall remembers an incident one Christmas Eve, when a lady, who happened to have only one leg, came into the store crowded with shoppers, and over the noise of the crowd shouted, "You sold me a pair of shoes . . . they're both for the same foot! And it's the wrong foot!" The Paschalls also recall the shortages everyone experienced during the Second World War when everything, especially coffee and sugar were in short supply. In 1955 they completely remodeled the store and added a grade-A snack bar, which served not only sandwiches, but also hamburgers and steaks. It became Paschall's Shopping Center. The Paschalls sold the business in 1971, and Hill Paschall went into the real estate business and moved to Franklin.

The Paschalls served all of Williamson County as well as the Arrington community. Benjamin Paschall served as magistrate on the county court for thirty years. Hill Paschall, his son, was also on the county court. At that time, all magistrates were justices of the peace and could perform marriage ceremonies as well as govern the community. During his younger days,

Leslie Waggoner house.

Hill Paschall served one year as a page in the state senate and another year as a page for the state house of representatives. He retired from the position of county commissioner because the Hatch Act would not allow him to serve as both postmaster and magistrate of the same community. Evelyn Paschall's brother R. G. Ray was elected to fill that position.

A school called Union Academy was started near the Arrington community before the Civil War. In 1851, Edwin Paschall, who came to Williamson County from North Carolina, bought land near the school to build a home, as he was to be the teacher. Paschall was also an editor of the *Western Weekly Review* in 1858 and 1859. His son-in-law Thomas Peebles followed Paschall as teacher. The school continued in operation after the Civil War with Alfred Wallace as teacher and Henry T. Crockett, assistant. Later, the primary school in the community was the Arrington School, which went through the eighth grade, and then students went onto College Grove or Franklin. Children growing up in Arrington spent many hours swimming in the nearby creek, riding horses, riding their bikes, and enjoying the uncomplicated life in the country.

Prominent churches in the area included the Trinity Methodist Church and the Bellview Cumberland Presbyterian Church. Arrington was also once the site of King's Chapel, one of the oldest brick churches in the county.

The Bellview Cumberland Presbyterian Church was founded in 1852 and started out as brush arbor and then tent meetings. For a brush arbor meeting, folks would clear a spot in the woods, make an auditorium out of the brush, and put planks down on the stumps to use as benches. The first minister was Rev. John McPherson, who preached for twenty-seven years without taking a penny for payment. McPherson also ran a private school near his home. Dr. B. H. Paschall was a member of the Bellview Cumberland Presbyterian Church and always had a habit of coming late to services. One Sunday, when the preacher called on him to offer a prayer, Dr. Paschall replied "I'm paying you to do the praying! You do the praying, I'll do the paying!"

Hopewell A. M. E. Church was started about 110 years ago on land bought from Tom Tulloss, off Wilson Pike and Duff Road, now known as Maple Lane. It was called "Rock Hill Circuit." After the original building burned, it was rebuilt and called "Hopewell."

One of the first churches in Williamson County was at Arrington. Called King's Chapel, it was a Methodist church built about 1815 under the direction of Bishop McKendree. Here, also, huge outdoor meetings were held at King's Campground by early ministers. Burials were started there in 1821 and continued until 1871 when the churchyard was filled. Time has erased and destroyed all but two gravesites.

One of Williamson County's earliest settlers and government officials, William Edmondson, is buried at King's Chapel. Edmondson served at the Battle of Kings Mountain in the Revolutionary War in 1783 and was awarded 320 acres of land in Williamson County in 1787. In 1799 he was one of the commissioners to erect public buildings for the new county of Williamson and was on the first jury at Franklin in 1800.

In 1849, the site of the Methodist church in this area was moved to Triune on Horton Highway. One of the later churches to come to the Arrington community was the Arrington Baptist Church. In 1963, there wasn't a Baptist church between College Grove and Franklin, and the Arrington congregation started as a tent meeting and then moved to the former Triune School. Property was secured on Highway 96 East in 1963, but it wasn't until 1967 that the actual building was constructed. The church was begun as a mission, sponsored by the Tusculum Hills Baptist Church of Nashville, but it became independent in 1968.

The Arrington community never had more than 200 residents and was about a mile all the way around. The old Paschall's Store building is now an antique shop and feed store. With the passing of time, Arrington has changed, and although it may be merely a wide point in the road, to the folks who have lived and grown up there, it will always be home.

4

Ash Grove

ASH GROVE, IN NORTHERN WILLIAMSON COUNTY, is a community which is no longer on the map, but several old homes and memories of the area's last covered bridge still remain. The community, in the Sneed Road area of Brentwood, took its name from the beautiful ash trees which once grew in the district.

The 1878 map of Williamson County lists homes built by three members of the Sawyer family in the Sneed Road area. Dempsey Sawyer's home was called "Rock Hill," Coston Sawyer named his homeplace "Locust Grove," and J. R. Sawyer owned "Locust Hill." Locust Hill has been restored by Robert Sawyer, while Rock Hill burned years ago.

The bridge over the Harpeth River at Ash Grove was built to ease trade between Davidson and Williamson Counties, hence the name "Union Bridge." The bridge was burned during the Civil War, but no one is sure if it was burned by Federal troops or by the people of the community to keep the enemy at bay. Due to lack of finances in the community, the bridge was not immediately replaced after the war. In 1881 a Mr. Fagan constructed a covered bridge. He used rock from fields in the area, and he covered the bridge with wood shingles. In the 1930s, Marshall Sawyer, Jere Sawyer, and Algie Sawyer all aided in recovering the bridge with tin. Teenagers were known to steal a kiss in the darkened tunnel and some Sunday evenings young boys would throw rocks through the bridge trying to make it to the other side without touching the sides of the bridge. Just as cars blow their horns going through the long tunnel nowadays, people would holler going

12

through the covered bridge, warning other buggy drivers they were coming through. In February 1948, the last covered bridge in the county came to an end when, after days of heavy rain, the old bridge, with piers weakened by the swollen river, sank into the waters of the Harpeth River. A modern steel and concrete structure on Sneed Road has replaced the bridge on what used to be called Union Bridge Road.

The only store in Ash Grove, on Ash Grove Road, now called Old Natchez Trace, was owned by John Stockett in the early 1900s. The business was run by Stockett and Walter Sweeney. The store was later bought by W. W. Miller, and his father John A. Miller worked there. Other owners included Joe Perry, Hatten Northern, a Mr. Reeves, and a Mr. Holt also ran the store before it closed in the 1920s. The store later burned to the ground, possibly when vagrants inhabited the building.

John Stockett, the original store owner, also had a sawmill behind the store which made rough lumber to build barns. One day, when a gentleman from Illinois was holding a revival meeting nearby, the boiler at the sawmill blew up, killing a mule, and scalding John Stockett's son Joe. After that, a tractor was used to work the mill and the boiler was never used again.

The intersection of Moran Road and Old Natchez Trace Road was the site of an early school, called the Old Moran Field School, on property owned by Sam Moran. Students attended school only six months out of the year, the other months were spent helping at home. Early teachers included Joe Bowman and John Miller, both Civil War veterans. Sometime in the 1890s the field school closed and the Ash Grove School opened.

The Ash Grove School went through the eighth grade. Teachers included Miss Wilma Cannon, Miss Julia Hayes, Miss Emma Mai Ring (this was her first teaching position in what was to be a long career teaching the county's young people), and Miss Pauline Parker. Emma Mai Ring first taught at the school in 1908 at the age of twenty. The school then was like many modern open classroom-style schools where students progressed at their own pace. The school closed in 1946.

The community of Ash Grove is situated on good river bottom land, which was then, as now, excellent soil for farming. Much of the food was shipped for sale into Nashville, first by wagon and later by train at Vaughns Gap.

Several churches, Pleasant Hill (also called Union Church) and later Ash Grove served the religious needs of the community. William Armstrong, an early settler, purchased land in the area on what was called Rocky Lane, just off Sneed Road. He called his home Pleasant Hill, after his

Remains of the last covered bridge over the Harpeth River.

home in Franklin County, Virginia. In 1813, his wife and his daughter, Sarah, gave land to start the first church in the community, and they also called the Presbyterian church Pleasant Hill.

Because there was no Methodist church in the area, some of the Methodists began worshiping at the Pleasant Hill Church, giving it the nickname "Union Church." These same Methodists soon felt the need for a church of their own. In 1848, William Armstrong Jr. and his wife Elizabeth gave land for what is now the Bethlehem Methodist Church. The Pleasant Hill Methodists, and the Methodists from Beech Grove, a church on Manley Lane, made up the congregation at Bethlehem Methodist.

Back in Ash Grove, the Pleasant Hill congregation decided to construct a second Presbyterian church. This became known as the Ash Grove Church. Land for the Ash Grove Church was given by Dempsey and Lucinda Sawyer, and the church became a member of the Cumberland Presbyterian denomination. The church was organized by Rev. Nathan F. Gill and was made up of descendants of early settlers, such as the Stockett, Armstrong, Sawyer, and Mose families. Henry H. Ring, a member of the Harpeth Presbyterian Church, liked to come over to Ash Grove and teach Sunday school.

What became of the Pleasant Hill and Ash Grove Church buildings? The Pleasant Hill Church was purchased by John Stockett, moved to his place on Stockett Road (now Vaughns Gap), and used as a granary. By 1967, the congregation at the Ash Grove Church had dwindled to between ten to fifteen people and the congregation disbanded. The General Assembly of the Methodist Church took over the building and sold it. The structure was eventually torn down, with some of the furnishings going to different churches. The organ went to a church in Dickson, and some of the furnishings were actually stolen.

Ash Grove didn't have a mail route until 1902, with mail coming from nearby Beechville. In 1902, Park Cotton became the first mail carrier. Doctors serving the small community included Dr. Felix Hill, Dr. A. D. Bradford, and Dr. John Sugg.

Ash Grove has become part of the Brentwood community, but descendants of original families still live in the area and enjoy reminiscences of the quiet times of Ash Grove.

5

Beechville

BEECHVILLE WAS ONCE AN ACTIVE COMMUNITY, although its name won't be found on any recent map of Williamson County. From 1800 until the early 1930s, Beechville was the community located on Hillsboro Road between Old Hickory Boulevard and south to Sneed Road. There were churches, several schools, at least three stores, a wagon stop, a post office and a blacksmith shop, and people who had a sense of family and caring, which make up any community.

The McCutcheons were the first important family to settle in the area, and there was a cabin located on what is now Harpeth Valley Farms. Samuel McCutcheon is said to have come down the river with the James Robertson party and the McCutcheon family lived in the area from the 1790s until the early 1930s. They were the first large landowners in the area and they gave the land for the Harpeth Presbyterian Church. The post office was located across the road from the church and in the same area was a mill, used for both a flour mill and sawmill.

Hillsboro Road itself was once a buffalo or Indian trail which wound its way to Leiper's Fork, and when Hillsboro Road was being built, the individual landowners would stand guard on their own property as the road went through.

Three stores were in the Beechville community. One of them was run by a Mrs. Allen, who was a Yankee sympathizer during the Civil War. Because of this, she was able to cross enemy lines into Nashville to purchase supplies which other stores found difficult to obtain, such as salt and kerosene. However, customers only came to her store as a last resort because she was an enemy sympathizer. Another store was located on the property which now belongs to the Battle Rodes family and was used as their guest house when it was no longer a store. The Rodes home burned in the mid-1960s, so they built their new home around the guest house. A third store became Beechville School, which was used from 1911 until 1954 to educate the black children in the community, and was the only school to utilize the Beechville name.

One of the earlier schools was built by one of the doctors in the community, Dr. Byrns, and his daughter taught school in the log cabin schoolhouse. It was called Ballou School and students would have their annual picnics near the Holly Tree Gap.

A very advanced school in Beechville was the Sunnyside School, located where the Greater Pleasant View Baptist Church now stands. There was the regular classroom, a dog trot, and a music room where the students increased their musical education. All the teachers were college graduates and the school ran from first grade through high school. In 1911 the school closed and students went to the Grassland School, which was then located on a hill overlooking Sneed Road and Hillsboro Road.

Before there was a formal church in the Beechville community, services were held at camp meeting grounds near what is now Johnson Chapel Road. The Harpeth Presbyterian Church was officially founded in 1811 by Gideon Blackburn, who founded it as a Presbyterian congregation. It was built on an existing congregation and it is the only institution in the community that is still going strong while the others have passed with time. There was also a Pleasant Hill Church which housed both the Presbyterian and Methodist congregations.

Doctors came into the Beechville community in the late nineteenth century when Dr. Byrns married one of the McCutcheon daughters and eventually fell heir to the McCutcheon property. When he was no longer able to practice medicine, Dr. Byrns was replaced by Dr. William James Parker who lived in a house on the corner of Beech Creek and Hillsboro Roads where the iris still bloom each spring. Dr. Parker had his office in his home. Two rooms were just off his front hall: one led to his parlor, the other to his office. Dr. Parker died at a young age having contracted pneumonia as a result of visiting a sick patient in the middle of a wet and rainy night. After Dr. Parker's death, Dr. John T. Sugg moved into the community, living in what had once been the local wagon stop, and picked up Dr. Parker's practice. In those days, doctors would practice their trade where they were needed.

Potato cellar on Lee-Rodes farm.

A blacksmith shop was also in Beechville and, during the Civil War, the only soldier shot in the community was a Yankee soldier shot right in front of the blacksmith shop. No one would touch or move the body but eventually other soldiers came to remove it.

The Beechville Tavern was located between Murray Lane and Beech Creek Road. Next to the tavern was a spring. When the tavern burned, the chimney was pulled into the spring. Years later Battle Rodes pulled the chimney out and found a perpetual spring. Today one can still see where the chimney had cut into the stone in the spring. Before the fire, the tavern served whiskey from gourds at a nickel or dime a gourd, depending on how thirsty a customer was.

The coming of the railroad through Middle Tennessee changed several things. It did not go through the Beechville community, and mail came from Brentwood, which eventually caused the Beechville post office to close.

What caused a once thriving community to disappear? During the 1920s, lawlessness and bootlegging became prevalent in the area. Many stills were in the wooded area of Beechville, and a nearby cave was used for dumping the body of a dead man. Also, the coming of automobiles changed the Beechville way of life. However, there are still a number of loyal families in the community who pride themselves on good schools, and churches, and a community way of life.

—————6—————

Bending Chestnut

COMMUNITY TOOK ITS NAME FROM
INDIAN METHOD OF MARKING TRAILS

T HE COMMUNITY OF BENDING CHESTNUT, located about ten miles west of Franklin, was named for the fact that Indians used to mark their trails by bending a chestnut sapling to the ground. One was near the crossroad of Bending Chestnut and Garrison Roads. One such chestnut was so large a buggy could pass under it.

The community had a one-room school, located just across the road from what is now Fox's Grocery Store on the corner of Bending Chestnut and Garrison Roads. The original school was knocked off its pillars when a cyclone went through the area in 1909. Cora Foster, a native of the Garrison community, was the teacher at the Bending Chestnut School from 1917 until 1949. In the early years, school started in July, and students were dismissed to help with the harvest in the fall.

Down Garrison Road about three miles was the Garrison School, another one-room schoolhouse, which had been built in the middle of a cattle field. It was painted with whitewash, to which someone had added some salt. The cattle soon began licking the whitewash off the school building.

The Bending Chestnut School was used for many years as a church with all denominations represented. Will Irvin, a Presbyterian minister, would come from Nashville to Franklin on the Interurban, then take a Ford model truck out to Bending Chestnut, where he would preach for as little as fifteen cents a Sunday. Every year, on Mother's Day, folks would gather for the Homecoming meeting. Before the school was used as a church, people would hold a brush arbor meeting.

Bending Chestnut School.

The Fox family continues to be one of the mainstays of the community. Colley Fox and his father purchased the store in 1919 after World War I. They rented the building for two years and then purchased it in 1921. After Colley Fox's death in 1975, the store continues to be run by Mr. Fox's daughter, Jewel Anderson.

During the thirties and forties, the store was Saturday night's entertainment spot. Folks would come in and sit on nail kegs, hay bales or feed sacks, and listen to the Saturday Night Fights or the Grand Ole Opry on a battery-operated radio. Electricity did not come to that part of Williamson County until 1947.

Telephones were also late in coming to Bending Chestnut. If someone needed to call a doctor, they went to one of the few phones in the area located at Harold Meacham's home on the Garrison Road. When a doctor came into the community, it would usually herald the arrival of a new baby. The Burns family had twenty-one children and a neighbor Mrs. Narciss Anderson was the community midwife and doctor, if one was unavailable.

One of the most remarkable people in the Bending Chestnut community was Charlie Swanson. He lived to be ninety years old, never married, had no formal schooling, never drove a car, and his home never had electricity. He was a blacksmith and a gunsmith and if he couldn't find a part for something he was repairing, he would make one. He was the self-sufficient type of person that kept the small community going.

As the name implies, the community was the site of a variety of trees, especially chestnut, and until the blight hit them in the 1930s, chestnut trees were used to build the beautiful split rail fences that dot the countryside. Harold Meacham once remarked that he found several new chestnut trees coming up and said they might be from the roots of the old trees which died some sixty years ago.

Sawmills have been the only industry for many years with trees once being used for railroad ties and barrel staves. Mules would haul the lumber into Hillsboro for transportation into Nashville. Fox's sawmill was started in 1953 by Gilbert and T. C. Fox Jr. Their primary product is lumber used by area farmers for their barns and storage buildings. Some lumber is sold to factories for furniture and hardwood flooring.

At the turn of the century, boys living in the area would catch wild calves, go fishing in nearby creeks, and work with mules; primarily, however, they would work on the farms. According to Harold Meacham, during the winter months, farmers would use their mules to haul dead trees out of the woods, and this would keep the mules in shape for the spring plowing and planting. Meacham also grew an unusual crop in his farm. He grew buckwheat which he said was good to feed the bees because it would make the honey extra dark and rich.

The Natchez Trace runs very close to the Bending Chestnut community and the new parkway goes through the area. Garrison Creek was so named because army troops garrisoned there when the government was changing the road from an Indian trail to a road.

Gospel singing is a favorite in the Bending Chestnut community. When the Bending Chestnut School building was sold, the Fox boys started using it to practice what they loved to do best, sing gospel songs. What started out as a performance one summer evening has turned into a two-night event and, in the last years, crowds of 2500 people made this one of the largest gatherings in the area. The concert is free to everybody who enjoys an evening of good gospel music.

According to Gilbert Fox, Bending Chestnut and the surrounding area is made up of good folks who have always worked hard raising a portion of their living out of the ground. They are neighbors who help each other in good times and bad, and although the community has never had more than seventy-five people as inhabitants, they feel a closeness with each other. Many who have moved away will come back to buy a portion of land to remind them of life in a small, close-knit community like Bending Chestnut.

7

Berry Chapel

CHURCH OF CHRIST GAVE
COMMUNITY ITS NAME

A T BERRY CHAPEL, the church is the center of the community. In learning about what makes up a community, one thinks of schools, shops, churches, a post office, but primarily, a community is people. Berry Chapel began in the 1880s when the Church of Christ met in a one-room school, located at the corner of what is now Hillsboro Road and Spencer Creek Road, in Perkins School, which later became Parham School. One of the first baptisms came in 1885, when Fannie Haskins, a prominent member of the community, was baptized by Brother Felix W. Sowell.

The move from Perkins School came in 1895 when six-tenths of an acre was acquired on the corner of Berry Chapel and Hillsboro Roads. The land was donated by Berry Hamilton, and the church was named for him. Lumber for the building was given by Sarah Whitfield, niece of Mrs. Bazel Berry and a relative of Berry Hamilton and the church was constructed by Samuel Farnsworth, grandfather of Russell Farnsworth.

The church consisted of one room, all wood, with wood-burning heaters and handmade pews. Early contributions ranged from $.45 to $3.50 a Sunday. Items of expense in the first church consisted of payments to the preacher, coal-oil lamps, and chimney-cleaning wicks. The original deed states if the building ever ceased to be used as a church, the land would return to the owner. The deed also mentions that the church name is Berry Chapel, not Berrys as it has been called for so many years because, realistically, it does not belong to the Berrys. A baptistry was not included in the first church, nor was there one when the congregation met at the school, so new members were baptized in the Harpeth River. In the early days, many country churches held services irregularly because of unheated buildings and sometimes the preachers were in charge of several churches. Some of the original preachers at Berry Chapel Church included F. W. Sowell, F. W. Smith, and L. C. Smith. F. W. Smith was the regular preacher at Fourth Avenue Church of Christ in Franklin and he traveled to Berry Chapel to preach their dedication service in 1895.

Perkins School, the original church, was either razed or moved when Hillsboro Road was rerouted in 1939. In 1953, Berry Chapel Church was completely renovated, with most of the work being done by members of the congregation and subcontractors. By 1962, the church had outgrown its location, and a neighbor, Matt Dobson Jr. and his wife, gave the church an additional acre of land, where the educational building was built in 1963. In 1964, tragedy struck when a fire completely destroyed the main church building, leaving only the new educational building standing. Undaunted, the congregation completely rebuilt the church and had their dedication services in September of 1965. Unlike larger Churches of Christ, elders and

Grimes house, built in 1826 by the Young family.

deacons were not appointed at Berry Chapel until 1965.

Looking back to the early 1900s, there was also a blacksmith shop in the area, run by Dan Campbell and situated where the Dark Horse Saddlery is now located. C. H. Hoskins also lived in the area before the Civil War and was a school teacher. During the war he served in the Confederate army in Company F of the Fourth Tennessee Cavalry, fighting in many principle battles of the war. When he returned to Williamson County, he turned to farming. Other early families included the Gatlins, Stanleys, Gardners, and the Whitefields. While Berry Chapel may not be a full-fledged community, being a portion of the Grassland area, it has a strong church with a strong, dedicated congregation which has grown and prospered over the years.

8

Bethesda

T HE COMMUNITY OF BETHESDA, situated southeast of Franklin, dates back to Revolutionary War days when pioneers from Virginia and North Carolina took up grants of land for their services in the war and bought property with an eye to making this area their new home. Sources differ on the meaning of the word "Bethesda": one says it comes from the Aramaic language meaning "House of Mercy"; the other, "Flowing Springs." In either case, it is a quiet, comfortable place to live.

Indians were the earliest inhabitants of the area, and early families who settled in the late eighteenth century include the Bonds, Alexanders, Steeles, Sprotts, Grigsbys, and Chapmans. Blythe Sprott served in the War of 1812 as well as the Creek Indian War while living in Bethesda.

The Civil War involved residents in the area who served with Tennessee regiments, but the war also came to their back door as in one incident which occurred at the William Steele House. Steele, a soldier with the Fourth Tennessee Cavalry, came home to Bethesda for a visit with his family. When the Federal soldiers learned of his presence, they came banging on the front door of his home in the middle of the night. His wife leapt out of bed and her husband crawled between it and the feather tick. She then quickly placed her three little boys into the bed and tucked them in. She ran to the door, opened it, and soldiers pushed passed her and began searching the house. They felt the small boys in the bed but never discovered Steele's hiding place in the same bed.

The first church, Bethesda Methodist Church, was organized in 1832 as a log structure. In 1844, a more permanent brick building was constructed

26

Bethesda Methodist Church.

to serve the worshipers. This building was either lost to a tornado or the ravages of the Civil War. In any case, a white-frame building was erected on the same location in 1870 and used as a church for ninety years.

The Bethesda Presbyterian Church, an offspring of the New Hope Presbyterian Church in the Harpeth community, was built in November 1879, and members held their organizational meeting in the Methodist church. The Presbyterian church was constructed with two front doors, one for the men and one for the women. Mrs. Leo Bond, a longtime resident of the community, recalls her parents always entered through the designated doors and never sat together during the services. Sunday schools at both churches would meet together, meeting the first and third Sundays at the Presbyterian church and alternate weeks at the Methodist church. In the 1930s, the Epworth League of the Methodist Church put on plays, hauling actors and costumes in the back of a large truck to take their productions to neighborhood schools.

Schools at the beginning of the century were on a pay-as-you-go system, with public schools coming later. Boys attended school in the winter, the girls in the summer, so the boys could help in the fields. The high school, an early public school, became accredited in 1929 and also housed an early post office. P. D. Scales and Bob Daniels served the Bethesda community as two of the early postmasters. The high school burned in 1935 when students were getting ready to put on a play. There was a short in the lighting system and fortunately it occurred before the actual production so no one was injured. The school PTA built the first gymnasium on the school grounds with the men furnishing the lumber. Bethesda can boast of having the first county school bus. They bought an old car from Marshall Cook, probably an old Cadillac, and converted it into a school bus. Harry Grigsby was the first school bus driver, carrying ten to twelve children to school from the Arno/Peytonsville area.

Community clubs played a very important role in Bethesda, with everyone participating. They sponsored home improvement, built a gym for the new elementary school, operated the school bus, and each summer they would have a community fair. Girls displayed clothing they had made, canned goods they had put up, and boys showed farm products. Winning items went to the county fair and some went to the state fair.

There were also 4-H Clubs in the community and, as today, club members would go to 4-H camp. These camps were held in schools, and children would not only bring their own sleeping equipment, they brought their own food, including live chickens, which were prepared outside the school, as this preceded the days of school cafeterias. A Boy Scout troop was also part of the community, led by the late Mr. Herbert McCall. His troop produced two Eagle Scouts.

When the Bethesda community was at its peak in the early 1900s, it boasted of a stove foundry, flour mill, saddle factory, sorghum mill, and cotton gin. There was even a casket shop and chair and bed factory. The chair factory created the Waddey straight-backed chairs and most of the older homes still have a Waddey chair which was handed down to family members.

The Bethesda Masonic Hall is the second oldest in the county. When the schoolhouse burned in 1935, children met in the Masonic Hall. Little children, so as not to disturb the older ones, would enter and leave the building through the windows, which they loved doing.

The community is dotted with small log homes, most of them originally slave cabins. There is one small-frame house, near the Alexander house on Bethesda Road, which was used during a smallpox epidemic early in the century. One entire family was housed in this small cabin with one person from the outside to attend to all their needs.

Bethesda has produced citizens prominent in the religious, educational, and medical fields. The grandfather of Tennessee Governor Henry Horton is from Bethesda. Three prominent physicians, Dr. Blythe Core, Dr. Jonathon Core, and Dr. William Clyde Eggleston were from Bethesda, and in the Grigsby family, there are at least six teachers. To this day, Bethesda is noted for its fine dairy and beef cattle farms and a strong sense of family ties which carry on through the generations.

9

Bingham

CHURCH AT BINGHAM
CALLED HOG EYE

THE BINGHAM COMMUNITY BEARS A FAMILY NAME for four members of the Bingham family who had homes situated close to each other on Old Hillsboro and Parker Branch Roads. Three of these homes, belonging to William J., James Jay, and William F. Bingham are still lived in today. The home of John T. Bingham has been replaced by a modern structure. Tax records indicate the Binghams began paying taxes in Williamson County around 1831. James Jay Bingham came to the county in 1827, and in 1831, was taxed for 98 3/4 acres, one free person, and one slave. His brother William J. Bingham was taxed for 293 acres at $800 and one slave at $600. Two of James Jay Bingham's children, William F. and John T., lived all their lives in Bingham. James Jay Bingham was born in 1800, his brother William J. Bingham was born in 1802. Both died in 1876. In addition to members of the Bingham families, other early settlers included the Waddell, Sweeney, Boyd, Carter, Maury, Stone, Poynor, Peach, Atkinson, Short, and Haley families.

The church at Bingham, organized in 1854, was of the Cumberland Presbyterian denomination, but at Sunday evening services, it was non-denominational, with Methodists, Presbyterians, and Church of Christ members all joining in the worship service. The church had the unusual name of Hog Eye because the floors had holes in the boards and the children could look down and see the pigs sleeping comfortably under the building. The first minister at the Hog Eye Church was Rev. John W. Williams of Arrington, who came to preach once a month. W. T. Stephens, father of Bud Stephens of the well-known gospel-singing Stephens Quartet

29

of Franklin, was a song leader at the church, and the little creek that mean-
ders by Parker Branch Road is called Hog Eye Creek.

Two schools served the community. The first was a log school located
near Charlie Gray's store on Old Hillsboro Road. Mollie Gray, Charlie's
mother, was the teacher. The other school, first called Beech Bottom
Academy, was located among the giant beech trees on the West Harpeth
River near Boyd's Mill. It began as a private school but later became a
public school, with one teacher for all twelve grades.

Bingham obtained its first post office in 1884. The first postmaster was
Thomas R. Bingham who operated a store and lived on a farm known as the
Clint Shaw farm. This post office was used for many years until Bingham
became part of a rural Franklin route. The first route carrier was Carey
Reynolds, and his mail was brought from Franklin to the Bingham store
daily. This store later became known as May's Store.

Around 1910, Charlie Gray's store, which had been built from material
salvaged from the demolished Fernvale Hotel, replaced May's as the predomi-
nant general store. Charlie sold farm equipment, furniture, and general
supplies, and he was also a smart merchandiser. He would attend fire sales,
collect salvage goods, and stretch them out to dry on a line in front of the
store. People came from Franklin and surrounding areas to get in on the bar-
gain merchandise. Another store which served the community, along with
Gray's, was Short's Store. The blacksmith shop, run by George Hughes and
Joe Blankenship, took in repair work the farmers could not do themselves.

One longtime resident of the community, Miss Sue Owen, was raised on
the farm which had been owned by the family of Matthew Fontaine Maury,
called the "Pathfinder of the Seas," when his father first came to Tennessee
from Virginia. When Sue's parents were married, the community held an
"Infare," or wedding reception, at May's Store for Will Owen and his young
bride. Sue Owen says she was a true tomboy and got into a lot of mischief
along with her brother Frank. Their father was a fifth-district magistrate
who also trained horses for a living. One day Sue, Frank, and some young
hired hands hitched up the horse-breaking cart, only this time they hitched
it to a steer calf. The steer took off running and ran headlong over a cliff,
with the children still in the cart. Older hands came running to the rescue,
took the children to safety, repaired the cart, and put it back in the barn.
When Will Owen came to use it, he wondered what happened. No one said
a word, and as the children were unhurt, he never knew of the incident.

Gray's Store at Boyd's Mill and Old Hillsboro Road.

The original Carter house, built by Francis Watkins Carter, was built on Waddell Hollow Road in Bingham around 1806. Francis was the father of Fountain Branch Carter, builder of the famous Carter House on Columbia Avenue in Franklin.

A notable landmark in the community was Boyd's Mill, built on the West Harpeth River around 1850. Men would come by wagon and horseback to have the miller grind their grain, and whittle or gossip while the great stones ground the produce. Jesse Short ran the mill after the Boyd family, and today the large stone foundation by the river can still be seen.

A covered wooden bridge was used to cross the Harpeth River at Boyd Mill Pike. During the Civil War, the river was up one day and a Yankee soldier was trying to cross it on horseback. There was a hole right by the bridge where horse and rider fell in and drowned in the swollen river. For many years, children in the area were warned not to fall into the "Yankee hole." The wooden bridge had planks which would make an unusual plunking sound and children liked to think there were ghosts on the bridge.

One little-known enterprise in the area was a federally licensed distillery, located on Stillhouse Hollow Road. It converted mountain water and corn mash into fine mountain dew. At one time an old fat goose would wander through the still and lick the sour mash drippings. It was a very happy, slightly inebriated goose.

An early physician was Dr. A. B. Poynor who married Millie Tunstall Bingham in 1860. His home is still standing on Old Hillsboro Road and has been restored. Poynor chairs are furniture items unique to the county. They were made by Dick Poynor, a black man who belonged to Dr. Poynor's father. The chairs were made of green maple, the rungs of seasoned oak, the slots of seasoned maple, and the splits of hickory strips. A lumber company in Bingham was run by Red Lehew, father of Franklin's Calvin Lehew, and was in business until the mid-1950s. Then Lem Parker served as a carpenter and coffin maker for the community.

The rural community of Bingham, as with so many others, has faded with the coming of the car and better roads, but there are still folks interested in the history of communities like Bingham and the families who first settled there.

─────10─────

Boston

EARLY SETTLER BORN IN A
FORT NASHBOROUGH STABLE

NOT ANYONE IS EXACTLY SURE HOW THE BOSTON COMMUNITY, situated off Old Hillsboro Road, from Mobleys Cut road to Davis Hollow Road, got its name. But legend has it that early settlers, standing on a nearby ridge, looked down at the low ground and said "it looks just like Boston," meaning Massachusetts. Families prominent in the settling of Boston include the Sparkman, Robinson, Skelly, Prowell, Marlin, and Sudberry families.

Seth Sparkman, the man most responsible for the settlement of Boston, was born in a stable near Fort Nashborough on a cold January night in 1797 when his parents were moving here from North Carolina. In 1801, Seth came with his parents to what was then the Second and Third Civil Districts of the county to 274 acres at the edge of a large Indian settlement. In 1812, volunteers were asked to join the army of General Andrew Jackson to fight the British. Both William and fifteen-year-old-son Seth wanted to be part of the action but someone needed to stay home. So, they drew lots, and William served at the Battle of New Orleans before returning to the Boston community. Seth grew to be one of the most industrious men in the county. In addition to farming, Seth Sparkman also operated a nursery, a woodworking shop, tannery, apiary, slaughterhouse, country store, and a post office. He also ran a saddlery where he made saddles for the Confederate army. In 1854, he donated land for what is now the second oldest church in the county, the Boston Church of Christ. The land was to be used to build a house of worship, and the deed stipulated that if for any time period of five to ten years it was not used for this purpose, it was to revert to the Sparkman heirs.

In 1858, he also donated the land for Boston's one-room school, to be located on the church grounds. In later years, if there was a funeral while school was in session, students were dismissed from school to attend the funeral service. Seth Sparkman and his wife Rebecca were not only pioneers in the settling of the community, according to the inscription on their tombstone, they were the first two people south of Nashville to be "baptized for the remission of their sins," and they were baptized by the famous Church of Christ preacher, Andrew Craig.

The one and only store in the Boston community is the one on Old Hillsboro Road now owned by the Pete Davis family. It was started by Lewis Hawkins on a road that paralleled the Boston Creek. Hawkins sold the store to Moses Carlisle, who ran the business for forty-two years. During that time, he had a livestock scale at the store where farmers would weigh their animals, then oftentimes drive them on foot to Franklin to be transported to the market in Nashville. The Middle Tennessee Railroad ran through the community, and when it was discontinued in the late 1920s, the county made the railroad tracks into the road, changing the direction of Old Hillsboro Road. As a result, Moses Carlisle put his store up on rollers and had it moved to its present location. The store burned in the 1930s but was rebuilt. Carlisle eventually sold the business to Clint Robinson, who in turn sold it to Pete Davis.

Tragedy came to the small community on April 29, 1909, in the form of a cyclone. It took the lives of several members of the Marlin family, eighteen-year-old Wilburn Marlin, Carrol Marlin, thirteen, and Freedi Marlin, age ten. Mrs. Finis Marlin died May 4 from her injuries. Goldy Coleman, a carpenter who had been working in the area and staying at the Marlin home, was also killed, as was thirty-year-old Gerdy Sweeney. A black woman, Nellie Murray, was killed along with her four-day-old baby.

The Boston post office was in the general store, at both locations, and mail was brought to the community from Thompson Station. Carlisle was one of the early postmasters and two of the substitute mailmen were brothers Roy and Clark Robinson. Clark would make his rounds on his trusty motorcycle, but early mail carriers started out with the horse and buggy. Other businesses in the community included two blacksmith shops, one run by Henry Warf, the other by Charlie Brown. Brown also owned the

Pete Davis' store.

community gristmill. Farmers usually brought their corn to the local mill but took their wheat into Franklin to Lillie Mill.

The Boston school, located on the church grounds, operated as first a one-room school, then a room was added in later years. One of the most memorable teachers was Dan Bates, who taught when Fred J. Page was superintendent of schools. The school first held eight grades, and later went up to the tenth grade. Students continued their education at Hillsboro High School. The Boston school operated until 1956. Children growing up in Boston liked to wade in the creek in the summer, and would skate, using their shoes as skates much to the consternation of their mothers, on the creek in the winter.

In addition to the usual crops and livestock, some farmers had apple orchards. Henry Warf would make cool refreshing apple cider to serve to friends and neighbors during the summer, then store the cider in barrels, letting it ferment into vinegar over the winter. The vinegar was used by the ladies of Boston for canning and preserving during the summer and the first cold days of the winter when they canned meat from the hog killings.

Small communities are self-sufficient, and Matt Sparkman was the local casket maker. His granddaughter Gladys House remembers helping him line the caskets with cotton and flannel padding. Matt's wife Sally Sparkman made the loaf for Sunday church services and she passed the tradition onto her daughter Lucy Sparkman Marlin.

The father of Ruby Peach was the last remaining Sparkman son and with his death, the name passed from the community. The Boston Church of Christ membership is made up primarily of the older generation, and what will become of the church if younger members are not there to carry on the tradition is a question often asked in not only Boston, but in all other small communities.

————11————

Brentwood

BRENTWOOD WAS A FORT
CALLED MAYFIELD STATION

P OPULATION IN BRENTWOOD, since the mid-1960s, has literally exploded. One of the fastest growing areas in the county, Brentwood is right on the county line between Williamson and Davidson Counties. For years a community of magnificent homes and illustrious names, it now includes modern shopping centers, top-flight restaurants, speciality shops, expanding office complexes, and a forward-thinking city government. Brentwood has grown by leaps and bounds, but some businesses which have been a part of Brentwood for several generations continue to serve the community. One such business is Huff's Grocery, which started in 1949 on Hardscuffle Road, and today is housed in a modern structure just across the street. Noble's started in 1929 as a drugstore on Franklin Road and became a restaurant in 1947. Even though the ownership changed, the Nobles retained ownership until 1985, when it became Boston's. However the Noble family still owns Travelers Rest Motel, next door to the restaurant.

The community probably took its name from the home of an early settler Horace McNish who lived in the area from 1827 until 1850. McNish had ancestral homes in Virginia called Woodstock and Brenton, and his mother was a descendent of a Virginia family named Brent.

The first white settlers in Brentwood were the Mayfields, coming to the area around 1780, and settling on what is now Old Smyrna Road and Wilson Pike. They built a fort for their family and neighbors. Other early settlers include the Sneed, Edmondson, Moore, Hunt, Crockett, Holt, Herbert, Frost, Hadley, and McGavock families. The Frost family came to the area around 1810, and settled at what became known as Cotton Port, the first business area in Brentwood with a gristmill, post office, cotton mill, and general store.

Brentwood abounds in historic homes and families. Two, Mayfield and Cotton Port, both on Old Smyrna Road, stand in tribute to the earliest settlers. Other notable homes include Forge Seat, on the corner of Wilson Pike and Crockett Road, which was built in 1808 by Andrew Crockett. The Crocketts operated an iron forge on the land and Andrew Jackson, on his way to New Orleans in 1812, stopped by to purchase arms for his men. Mooreland, now the centerpiece for the Koger Center on Franklin Road, was begun in 1846, completed several years later, and used as a hospital by both Union and Confederate armies after the Battle of Nashville. Midway, home of the Brentwood Country Club, was built by Lysander McGavock in 1829 and takes its name from being halfway between Franklin and Nashville.

The Sneed family has been a strong part of the Brentwood heritage since the coming of James Sneed and his wife Bethenia Hardens Perkins Sneed to the area in 1798. He built a one-room log cabin on Old Smyrna Road, the first of many homes to be built by members of the Sneed family. Those include Windy Hill on Old Smyrna Road, Foxview, Brentvale, and Valley View Farm. Valley View was the lifelong home of the late Mary Sneed Jones, where Brentwood's first post office building is still standing.

The first schools in Brentwood were plantation schools, where children were taught in the family homes. Boiling Springs Academy on Moores Lane was started in 1833 and took its name from a spring across the road. Classes were taught in orthography (another word for spelling), reading, writing, arithmetic, Latin, Greek, English, and the sciences. It was also a boarding school for students away from home. The school continued in operation until the turn of the century and is still standing on Moores Lane.

Lipscomb Elementary School on Concord Road was founded in the late 1860s by William Lipscomb, brother of the founder of David Lipscomb School in Nashville. The first building was a log structure, and students came from Kentucky and Alabama as well as Middle Tennessee. The county took over the school, and in 1949 a new building was constructed. This burned in 1958 and the present structure, on the site of William Lipscomb's original log school, was built in 1959.

Brentwood now has numerous public and private schools, including Brentwood Academy on Granny White Pike, Brentwood High School and Brentwood Middle School on Murray Lane, and W. P. Scales Elementary

School on Holly Tree Gap Road. All these schools have come into existence since 1965, an example of the rapid growth of the community.

The first church in the area was Liberty Church, founded in 1800 by Green Hill, a Revolutionary War veteran and Methodist leader. The church is located on Concord Road, and in 1808 it hosted the Western Conference of the Methodist Church, the first such conference held west of the Alleghenies.

Owen Chapel Church of Christ was organized in 1859 and was known as Euclid Church. The church is named for James C. Owen who donated the land and helped erect the building on Franklin Road. The original roof, with the exception of a portion damaged in a tornado of 1869, as well as the pews and wooden partitions, is still part of the building. The two front doors, one for the men and one for the women, are still in use, and the church has been in continuous use since 1859 with the exception of several times during the Civil War when Federal troops were foraging in the area.

Johnson Chapel off High Lea Road was constructed on its present site in 1925, but the church was established in the early 1800s and in the early days people camped on the grounds during religious meetings. Matthew Johnston purchased land on the Little Harpeth River where he built a small church and called it Johnston's Chapel. The name was later changed to Johnson. The first church building was a log structure and baptisms were held in cool water nearby. The log church is supposed to have burned around 1850. It was followed by a weatherboard building which was torn down in 1925 to make way for the present structure.

Brentwood Methodist Church is a beautiful building with a majestic spire and richly colored stained glass windows overlooking busy Franklin Road. The church was first a two-story structure on Hardscuffle Road with the first floor used as a school and the second floor used for church services. It was also the first Methodist church in the country to allow men and women to sit together during worship services. This historic vote came in 1859. In 1884 the church building was destroyed by a windstorm and the congregation built a new church on Church Street. This building burned in 1936 and again the congregation rebuilt and stayed in that location until the current church was built in 1972. Other Brentwood churches include the Mt. Lebanon Missionary Baptist Church, the Brooks Memorial Church, Smyrna Church, Episcopal Church of the Advent, Concord Road Church of Christ, the New Hope Community Church, and the Lords Chapel.

The first post office to serve the community was probably at Cotton Port, the Frost property on Old Smyrna Road. The Good Springs Post Office

Mooreland, one of Brentwood's many historic homes.

was the first official post office in 1827 and was located on Franklin Road. The building which now stands in the yard of the home belonging to the late Mary Sneed Jones on Wilson Pike was the first post office to be called "Brentwood," in 1856. The first rural postal route was set up by Sam Taylor in 1902. There have been several post office locations since 1856; the newest building on Brooks Chapel Road was opened in 1984.

In March 1863, following the Battle of Thompson Station, Union forces headed north, setting up camp at Brentwood. Brigadier General Nathan Bedford Forrest completely encircled two separate Federal camps, capturing 800 men and their valuable plunder. This was the last major fighting in Brentwood for two years, but the pillaging activities continued and few if any homesteads in the area were left untouched. The Civil War brought numerous skirmishes to the Brentwood area, but the area was primarily used for foraging expeditions by both the Union and Confederate troops.

Brentwood today has an array of restaurants from fast food to quality cuisine, but the first tavern and stagecoach inn was operated by Collin McDaniel in 1808, near the entrance to what is now the Stonehenge subdivision on Franklin Road. He also served for fourteen years as a magistrate of the county and was postmaster of the Good Springs Post Office.

Like all of Williamson County, Brentwood is a community steeped in the traditions of the past and looking forward to new traditions in the years ahead.

─────12─────

Burwood

COMMUNITY HAS GHOST
NAMED "CRAZY MARY"

THE COMMUNITY NOW KNOWN AS BURWOOD, on Carter's Creek Pike just west of Franklin, was initially called Williamsburg in honor of the Williams' family. The name was later changed to Shaw for another resident. Finally, James Drake Pope suggested the name Burwood from Mrs. Humphrey Ward's novel *Robert Elsmere*. Besides the Williams, Popes, and Shaws, early settlers include the Martin, Akin, and Murfree families.

The Reverend John Pope was a Williamson County taxpayer as early as 1805 on land grants given for service in the Revolutionary War, and his land was surrounded on three sides by Indian territory. He and his family cleared the land for growing their own supplies, and they built a distillery which was considered a saleable crop in those days. Pope was a circuit-riding Methodist preacher known as "Parson Pope," who wanted little to do with bishops and missions, setting his sights on reaching individual neighbors. In 1818, seeing the need for a church building, Pope deeded one-half acre of land to be used by any denomination or sect so long as they didn't infringe on someone else's beliefs. Large camp meetings which lasted for days were held on the church grounds, now called Pope's Chapel, and used by many denominations. The building was also used as a schoolhouse, and stood until 1910, when a tornado destroyed the structure. The church was rebuilt in 1912 as the Burwood United Methodist Church. John Pope's home, Eastview, is preserved in excellent condition today and owned by Jack L. Grigsby and Judy Grigsby Hayes.

The Burwood Church of Christ was built near the school as the West End Church of Christ and moved to its present location about 1914. Lawrence Grove Missionary Baptist Church is located at the intersection of Pope's Chapel Road; other churches include Jones Chapel Nazarene Church, Mount Calvary Missionary Baptist Church, and Leiper's Fork Primitive Baptist Church, better known as the "Old Brick Church" and seen upon entering Burwood on Carter's Creek Pike.

Burwood is home to a number of other churches. Although there is no Presbyterian church now, there was once one located on land now owned by Brown Cannon's family. It was moved up to Burwood and was located across from Huff's Store.

During the Civil War, Jake Martin Sr. organized a company of men at Burwood and Thompson Station which became part of General Nathan Bedford Forrest's Cavalry. He and his men helped destroy a railroad for the Yankees. Because of this, Federal troops burned Martin's home in Burwood.

In another incident during the Civil War, the grandson of Parson Pope, John Osborne Pope, was a young Confederate soldier trying to escape from the enemy and make it home. He did get back to the homeplace and hid in the attic. When a blue-clad soldier learned of his whereabouts, he tried to go after him. A family servant spotted the Yankee coming and quickly grabbed a basket of apples she was going to preserve for the winter. She immediately began scattering them on the steps leading to the hiding place. She was a 250-pound woman who stood at the foot of the steps, hands on her hips and dared the soldier to pass her and ruin the apples. The Yankee soldier left, leaving young Pope safe in the attic.

The earliest store in Burwood was run by Dr. Williams' son, Eddie, and daughter, Mrs. Hill Church. Later came the store run by the Shaw family, for whom the town had earlier been named, and the present Huff's Store was once run by the Akin family. Today, Huff's Store is still the town gathering place and still has two rolling ladders, which must be two of the last ones in the country, used to reach produce on the upper shelves. The store has a large stairway leading to the second story where shoes and clothing were for sale.

Before the days of drugstores, country doctors used to mix their pre-scriptions at the back of the store, then dispense them to waiting patients on their route. The post office was housed in the general store, but was closed around 1922 and mail came from Thompson Station.

At one time, Carter's Creek Pike was a toll road, with the tollhouse located near the old brick church. Toll was five cents for horses, ten cents

Huff's Store.

for buggies, fifteen cents for loaded wagons, and walkers could crawl under for free.

West End School, built on Pope's Chapel Road, was a two-teacher school until it was closed in 1916. The building is still preserved on the Eastview farm where a blackboard and the stage used for the children's productions still exist.

A large-frame school was built in 1913, just across from the store on land donated by Vance Akin. Well-known educator Miss Emma Mai Ring served as principal at the three-room school in 1920. The building was used until 1956 when it was replaced by a brick structure. Students from the frame school were allowed to each place one brick in the new school. A one-teacher school, Sycamore, also served many community residents until its closing.

At one time, Cayce Springs was a resort area in the Burwood community, with a hotel and cabins where people would come from all over to partake of the sulphur and mineral spring waters for medicinal purposes. Leonard Grigsby remembered when his grandfather rode his horse to Cayce Springs for his Confederate soldiers' reunion.

Among the businesses that once served the Burwood community and are no longer there are the blacksmiths. At one time there were two blacksmith shops, one run by Dan Hicks and the other by Bill Huff. There was also a community creamery which became a barber shop.

Besides stores, churches, and beautiful homes, Burwood also has a resident ghost. Crazy Mary, as she is called, is said to still haunt the Leonard Grigsby house, which is now known as the House of Lights, because so often lights can be seen where none are on. Some who attended the old West End School remember seeing what looked like a snowfall on an early autumn day, when it was really Crazy Mary shaking all the feathers out of her featherbed. Another time, she was spotted sitting in the cold spring water. Crazy Mary, or her ghost, has never harmed anyone, but her presence, and that of the old Pope-Helm Cemetery 150 feet from the Grigsby house, offered Judy Grigsby Hayes a wonderful opportunity to scare some of her visiting city friends when she was growing up in Burwood. For a relatively small community, there are a number of cemeteries. Besides the Pope-Helm Cemetery, there is the Martin Cemetery, the Jones Community Cemetery on Sycamore Road, and the Burwood Community Cemetery on Carter's Creek Pike.

Some names in Burwood have been there a number of years such as Fly, Lavender, Jones, Sparkman, Cannon, Huff, Dodd, Southall, Byrd, and many others. Folks in the community would get together each summer for community fairs, with contests, exhibits of home canned goods, and a chance to greet their neighbors. One year, Mrs. Annie Jones was a grand winner of the hog-calling contest. In later years there was also a Ride-A-Thon, starting about 1946 and instigated by the late O. A. Sparkman and the late J. R. Lavender, who brought folks from far and wide to ride their horses for about ten miles together and return to Burwood School for a barbecue lunch and an afternoon filled with baseball games, sack races, mule pullings, and prizes.

According to Judy Grigsby Hayes, "Burwood is a pretty, quiet, peaceful and unspoiled retreat, away from the noise and rushing of the city and a place where folks still know and care about each other and are ready to help in time of need. Once you've grown up in Burwood, no other place is quite as good . . . you look forward to coming home again. Burwood . . . my home filled with my friends."

────── 13 ──────

Callie

THE COMMUNITY OF CALLIE, located about six miles south of Franklin just off Lewisburg Pike, was named for Callie McMillan, youngest daughter of Jim McMillan, who ran the general store from 1893 until 1902. The store also served as a local post office, with Dee Page as one of the Franklin mailmen who took the mail to the Callie Store. People had to travel to the store to get their mail before the days of mail routes. In 1907, Sam Edgmon moved the store about 150 yards down the road where he continued to operate it as a general store, and he also operated a market. Besides the post office, the store also housed the community blacksmith shop, and at one time, the store was the scene of community dances with Howard Hood Sr. playing the fiddle and Bert Guffee accompanying him on another instrument.

There were no schools in the Callie community, students went through the first eight grades at either the Douglas School on Hen Peck Lane, or Harpeth School on Lewisburg Pike.

Lewisburg Pike, like most major roads in the area, was once a turnpike, with the tollgate first located a mile south of Franklin. It was moved to the Stoddard farm, a mile past Callie, then moved again to a location across from the Cowles Chapel Church. Logan Hood ran the tollgate on the Stoddard farm; Buck Fleming was the tollgate keeper at the Cowles Chapel location. Beale Lane came into the Callie community from Peytonsville Road, but ceased to exist around 1900.

When the post office was torn down, lumber from the building was used to make a chicken house on Howard Hood Sr.'s farm. James William Hood has this weather-worn board with the original Callie mail slot, smoothed with age and the passing through it of many pieces of mail.

At one time there was a spring on the west side of the road near the Callie Store. A pipe ran under Highway 431 from the spring to a watering trough on the east side of the road. When Lewisburg Pike was widened in the 1940s, the pipe was still there and the spring still running. When plans were first made for Interstate 65, it was supposed to run right through the Callie Store, but the plans were changed to its present location.

Families in the Callie community included the Hoods, McMillans, and Edgmons, and at one time, there were twenty Hoods on Route 2. The Callie community was a small portion of Williamson County, with only a few families making up the entire community. There are few reminders of a quieter, simpler way of life, but the families who still live in the area remember and want to pass their memories onto future generations.

—————14—————

Clovercroft

NAMED FOR
FIELDS OF CLOVER

T HE CLOVERCROFT COMMUNITY, nestled along Wilson Pike, was named by Mrs. Will Paschall, wife of Dr. William Andrew Paschall, who practiced in the area in the 1890s. Mrs. Paschall took the name Clovercroft from the vast amounts of clover growing in the fields and the word "croft" is used by the English and Scotch to mean "a small area." The community got its name about 1902, when there was a post office in the area.

Before the area was officially named, Wilson Pike was created and built by slave labor, running from Brentwood to Arrington. James H. Wilson traveled to Mississippi for the slaves who in turn built the road which was used as a toll road.

Blind Joe Wilson, one of the most prominent men in the Clovercroft community, was in the process of building his home during the Civil War when Yankee soldiers threatened to burn the house if he continued to work on it. He ceased construction until after the war and completed the residence in 1865. Even though he was blind, he could tell just by knocking on a board if it had a knot in it and would eliminate that plank. He also built the house with its back to the main road, saying when he finished it, he would change the direction of the road, which he did. It later passed in front of his home. Joseph Wilson, Blind Joe, was born blind, and lived from 1797 to 1881. He was a truly remarkable man. His father died when he was very young and he lived with an uncle, Jason Wilson, until he was seventeen. He made his fortune before the Civil War and at one time owned more

47

Entering Clovercroft. To the left, the Sheddy Wilson house.

than fifty slaves. At his death he owned 900 acres of land. According to his obituary, he was kind to the poor, charitable to all in distress, and a good neighbor. He died on the place where he was born, leaving behind a wife and eight children. One of his direct descendants, Joe D. Wilson of Franklin, was the last Wilson to leave Wilson Pike, when he moved to the Moores Lane area in 1980.

Early settlers in the Clovercroft area include the Wilson, Herbert, Shannon, Osborne, Cunningham, McArthur, Butts, Nolen, Crockett, Lewis, Whitfield, Pollard, Jones, MacMahon, Jamieson, and Seward families. The local blacksmith shop was run by J. W. Butts near the store and post office, and he operated the shop for thirty years. After Butts, it was run by Dude Merritt, who also kept the grounds at the Franklin Post Office. The two main churches, Jones Chapel Church of Christ and Trinity Methodist Church, are located on Wilson Pike. Before Trinity Methodist, the church was called Mount Zion and built on Burke Hollow Road.

During the Civil War, Yankee soldiers destroyed the Mount Zion Church and carried off the materials. After the war, the congregation went to work rebuilding on land bought from Thomas Cunningham. They bought two and one-half acres at $100 an acre. Trinity was built as a two-story building; the downstairs area was for the church and upstairs there were two rooms, the large room for a school, the smaller one for the Masonic Lodge. Their first pastor was A. F. Lawrence. From the years 1879 to 1887, there was no Sunday school during the winter months due to the cold weather and, in 1884, the Women's Missionary Society was founded. As today, the wheels of government grind exceedingly slow. In 1907, the federal government paid the congregation $1100 for the damage the soldiers had done to the Mount Zion Church in 1863. This money was used to build a parsonage. In 1909, a tornado whipped through the area blowing out both the north and east sides of the building. Earlier, in 1897, another tornado had blown off the second floor of the building.

Jones Chapel Church of Christ was started with a tent meeting around 1880, when S. M. Jones, a student at the Nashville Bible College, was preacher. Later, before a church was built, they met in church members' homes, one being Mrs. Cunningham. Jones Chapel experienced the same fate as did Trinity Methodist. The first church was blown away by a tornado and, while being rebuilt, a tornado again struck. The third time was the charm and the church is standing. When the present Jones Chapel was being built, John N. Jones was a teenager and he helped haul trees into Nolensville to the sawmill where they were turned into lumber for the church.

The Clovercroft community seemed to produce an above average number of doctors. Dr. Tom Pollard, Dr. Jack Seward, Dr. Beverly Toon Nolen, Dr. Douglas Seward, Dr. Hardy Hawkins, and Dr. Yvonne MacMahon. Dr. Joe Herbert grew up in Clovercroft, was educated in Philadelphia, and practiced in Arkansas. Dr. Will Paschall, whose wife named the community, gave up his practice early in life and began raising race horses. Another doctor for the community was Dr. J. W. Greer, grandfather of Dr. Fulton Greer.

The earliest school was the one atop Trinity Church. Another was built on the lot between the church and the present school on Wilson Pike. W. P. Scales, who went on to become a superintendent of Williamson County schools, was one of the early teachers at the Trinity School, which ran through the twelfth grade. Community events would take place at the school, where they had square dances and suppers. When there were ice cream suppers, the ice cream was transported by the Lewisburg & Northern Railway from Nashville to the Clovercroft station.

The railroad was started about 1910 and ran from Nashville to Decatur, Alabama. It ran twice a day. Folks could go into Nashville by train to shop in the morning, returning on the afternoon run. When the railroad was being constructed, a tent city was set up on the corner of Liberty Pike and Wilson Pike to house the railroad workers who consisted of many different nationalities.

One night, several Italians spotted some large birds circling in the sky. Thinking the birds were nice juicy chickens, they shot them, and roasted the birds for their evening meal. When the men became ill, Dr. Kirby Smith Howlett was called from Franklin. Only then did the men learn they had eaten buzzards.

The Clovercroft Store has been housed in several buildings, but always in the same location, where Clovercroft Road runs into Wilson Pike. It was leased to S. J. Wilson around 1910, and then operated by the Jamieson family. The building burned in the 1940s and this is the third structure. In recent years it has been run by Scott Stephens, and is currently being operated by Ray Locke under the name "Jamieson's Grocery."

The main thoroughfare, Wilson Pike, was a toll road with three tollgates. Horseback riders paid ten cents; a horse and buggy was charged fifteen cents. The first automobile was owned by S. J. Wilson who made the purchase because he hated chasing horses. It was a Model T, crank-style auto with Isenglass curtains that snapped inside, rather than glass windows.

Children enjoyed Saturday afternoon baseball games, and an occasional basketball game, which in the early 1900s was a new game. When Scales was at the school, he would not allow any of the girls to take part in the games. He thought it was not ladylike.

When Joe D. Wilson left Wilson Pike in 1980, it signaled the end of an era with a slower-paced lifestyle. However, there are still many beautiful homes along the Pike, with large shade trees and big yards, reminders of a simpler time in the Clovercroft community.

───────15───────

College Grove

ONCE CALLED POPLAR GROVE—LATER TOOK ITS
NAME FROM TWO SCHOOLS IN COMMUNITY

C OLLEGE GROVE STARTED AS A COMMUNITY AROUND 1800 when James Allison purchased 400 acres of land on Grove Creek in the southeast portion of the county. William and Mary Ogilvie came from North Carolina and settled nearby, and James Allison married one of the Ogilvie daughters. In the early years of the Ogilvie's stay in the community, the story is told that one night, when James and his family were dining, he looked up to find himself staring back at several Indians outside their window. The family quietly managed to finish their meal, then as suddenly as they came, the Indians left.

Two early settlers were Arch Hughes and a Mr. Rogers of North Carolina, settling on land deeded from Revolutionary War grants, around 1800. A home built by Hughes about a mile southwest of College Grove was constructed of brick made by slave labor of material on the property. It stood from 1824 until March 1925 when it was leveled by a tornado.

Another early settler was William Demonbreun, son of Timothy Demonbreun, an early Nashville settler who lived in a cave on the banks of the Cumberland River. Other settlers in the College Grove area include the Covington, Cannon, Webb, Page, Gentry, and Scales families.

From the late 1700s until 1840 the community then known as Poplar Grove was made up of large beautiful farms. Then in 1840, the main road, Horton Highway, was built as a toll road. Over the years, nearby farmers would keep the road in good repair using sand from the creek and working with horses, mules, and wagons.

The post office came to Poplar Grove in 1861, and the government told the settlers there was already a Poplar Grove, so the name was changed to College Grove in honor of the two schools, one for boys and one a female seminary, in the community. The boys' school, Cary and Winn Academy, was started just before the Civil War. It was a boarding school, and a former resident Jonnie Demonbreun remembered that boys coming from Columbia and surrounding areas would board in the house in which she now lives. It was also a subscription school with pupils being charged by the day—ten cents a day for the younger students and fifteen cents daily for the older boys. At the most, there were twenty-one to forty-two students, and, according to one record, the most the school ever took in at one time was twenty-one dollars. The College Grove Elementary School was located where the Cary and Winn Academy once stood. With the coming of the Civil War, the Cary and Winn Academy students and their teachers joined the Confederate forces. The war at one time came right to Mrs. Cary's home in College Grove. A badly wounded Yankee soldier was traveling by horseback and fell from his horse. Disregarding the color of his uniform, she had him carried to her house. His leg was almost shot off, and despite her efforts, he died in her home. He was buried in her garden until he could be moved to the National Cemetery in Nashville. Professor Cary was imprisoned in the North during the war, but was able to return to his teaching at the end of the hostilities. Professor Winn was killed in north Georgia in 1864. The academy was opened later as a public school and torn down in 1916.

Dr. Urban G. Owen was born at nearby Owen Hill and studied at the University of Pennsylvania and the University of New York. In 1858 he returned to College Grove to set up his medical practice, marrying sixteen-year-old Laura Dobson a year before the Civil War broke out. He enlisted in the Tennessee Regiment, along with other College Grove boys. Letters written from the field back to his young bride are still preserved in *Tennessee Historical Quarterly* magazines. His letters contained news of the College Grove contingent, including the fact that a number of their company came down with the mumps. His recurring request to the folks back home was the need for boots which never seemed to last. Although he moved with the regiment to neighboring counties such as Rutherford and Bedford as well as Chattanooga and North Georgia, he seemed to be much farther away. His letters during 1864 reported that many of the College Grove soldiers had deserted and were heading home. While Owen wrote his wife many letters between 1861 and 1864, he never told her about the battlefield conditions

House that was once behind Covington's Feed and Seed.

under which he had to perform surgery. Returning to College Grove after the war, he soon became known as "Old Doc Owen" with a reputation for keeping his horse saddled and ready for house calls even during church services. His office was attached to his home and he dispensed drugs there, the only place between Murfreesboro and Franklin they could be obtained.

Both the boys' school and the female seminary were located on church property. The boys' school was on land given by James P. Allison and joined property given for the Poplar Grove Cumberland Presbyterian Church, while land for the female seminary was sold by Dr. Samuel Webb to be used for the school and the Methodist church.

At one time, Sunday schools were held together at the Presbyterian and Methodist churches, and the house just behind Covington's Feed and Seed Mill was the Methodist parsonage before 1910.

The Poplar Grove Cumberland Presbyterian Church started in 1860 and was renamed College Grove Cumberland Presbyterian Church in 1861 when the community name changed. One hundred years later, in 1961, it became United Presbyterian Church, but this change only lasted five years because in 1966, the church was dissolved and the property reverted to the College Grove School which joined it.

The College Grove Church of Christ was started in 1922 and is now in its third building. The congregation first met in an old granary near the railroad tracks and later moved to a general store. The church, started by the Will Marable family, then moved to the basement of their present building in 1945, where they met until 1950 when the auditorium was completed.

The railroad, Lewisburg & Northern, came through about 1914 and residents remember the workers lived in a place called New Town. Jonnie Demonbreun recalls riding a stage coach that came from Chapel Hill through College Grove.

The Bank of College Grove, once the Nashville City Bank and now Dominion Bank, was chartered in 1911, and telephone service with the United Phone Company came in 1916. Powell Covington started Covington's Feed and Seed Mill in the mid-1930s. It was started in a store and moved to its present location in 1937. Maxwell's Pharmacy, the community gathering place, was started by the Maxwell Brothers early in the 1900s, and is now known as the College Grove Pharmacy, operated by Charles Rigsby.

At the school, the College Grove PTA was the first parent-teacher organization in the county. The College Grove Book Club was started in 1920 as a means for young mothers to socialize once a month and exchange books and ideas. Today, their method of reading and exchanging books is still in effect.

The College Grove area is a very active, vital part of the county, with beautiful, stately homes, some dating back to the Ogilvie, Demonbreun, and Allison families, which are still in good use today. There are still large family farms in the community, and friends gather for coffee, Cokes, or gossip at the College Grove Pharmacy in good weather and bad. The growth of the community has slowed over the years, but the caring attitude of neighbors for each other will never change.

16

Craigfield

COMMUNITY STARTED BY
VACHEL ISAIAH BARNHILL

THE SMALL COMMUNITY OF CRAIGFIELD is situated about twenty miles west of Franklin on Pinewood Road, just off Hillsboro Road. Its gently rolling countryside is suitable for cattle grazing, but there are very few row crops in the area. The community was started by Vachel Isaiah Barnhill about 1840, and named for the Craig place, a nearby farm which had a good spring for the family members and the livestock. Families living in the community around 1900 included the Barnhill, Sullivan, Forehand, Tidwell, Bradford, and Southern families.

The first school was a one-room log building, constructed sometime before the turn of the century, while a two-room school opened in 1912. One year there were 100 youngsters, some even coming from Hickman County, crowding into the two-room building, eager for education. They sat on benches, sometimes three to a bench. The school closed when consolidated schools came in around 1950. School years were different from what they are today. School doors were open from July to February, because many of the youngsters walked to school without shoes, and obviously, couldn't walk the distance in the winter months.

The community general store was built right next to the schoolhouse. The first owner was Joe O'Steen, and it was later run by Jim Overbey, first cousin to Glen Overbey, who for so many years had a store on Carter's Creek Pike.

School teachers in Craigfield had a way of teaching school and then buying this store. Joe O' Steen sold the store to Robert Turman who had been a teacher; he in turn sold it to Jim Overbey who had also been a teacher. Most of the store owners were raised outside the county, came in to teach, and then bought what has become known as Overbey's Store.

Another store in the community was built by J. D. Lampley, about a mile and a half south of Overbey's Store. It was run by L. D. Parham from 1951 until 1973. Norman Green took over after that and managed the business for about nine months, until it burned down in 1974.

There was no post office in Craigfield, but there was a large locked post box on the front of Overbey's Store. Mail carriers heading for Bon Aqua in one direction or Primm Springs in the other, would stop by the Craigfield post box, collect the letters heading in their direction, and deposit those going the other way. These rural mail carriers were the only ones with the keys to the post box. Mail coming into Craigfield itself came from Columbia.

A blacksmith shop was located in the area, although most of the men did their own "smithing." A mill run by John Hammond to grind corn was located just across from the store.

Boys growing up in Craigfield played baseball games each Saturday against other community ball teams, and Craigfield had one of the top-notch teams in the area. The boys also liked to ride their mules to church meetings during the summer months. The girls stayed home a lot and helped their mothers, but they always attended the church meetings.

One Fourth of July celebration in the 1920s, Jim Walker, a friend, and their girlfriends went for a ride in his Model T open-air car. On the country

Former store and post office.

road, Jim ran over a groundhog, whereupon the other boy got out of the car, picked up the dead animal and tied it with a rope to the back of the car.

They drove back to the Craigfield picnic, with the dead animal trailing behind the car. When they reached the picnic, someone removed the groundhog from behind the car, flung it in the air, and it landed in the lap of one of the girls in the car. Her date became so angry, he started punching the boy and a good old fashioned free-for-all broke out. One thirteen-year-old boy standing nearby was hit in the middle of his forehead with a whiskey bottle. The boy was Gilbert Sullivan, who was later sheriff of Williamson County and, until his death, the mark from the bottle stayed on his forehead. One of the regular events at the Fourth of July picnics was the greased pole climb, where energetic young men would climb up the pole to reach the dollar bill placed at the top.

Craigfield could boast of having a music teacher. Pink Daugherty would hold music classes during the winter months at nearby Union Valley Methodist Church, teaching the children their scales and how to read music. Mr. Southern was a furniture maker and had a mule-driven lathe for turning the rounds on the furniture. It was set up like the mule-driven equipment which makes sorghum.

The original church house, a chapel in Craigfield, was used by all denominations; anyone wanting to preach there was able to. This building was later used as the Free Will Baptist Church. There was also a Missionary Baptist Church, with the Church of Christ built on Vachel Barnhill's land about 1908. Church services were conducted several times a month, with the second Sunday of the month reserved for the Missionary Baptist Church and third Sunday services held at the Free Will Baptist Church.

Medical attention came in the form of doctors on horseback. The first was Dr. Cox. He was replaced by Dr. Hensley, who rode up from Maury County. Hensley served the community until Dr. Raymond came during the First World War. All the doctors carried their medicines with them, the most popular medicinal remedy being a dose of soda.

Electricity came to Craigfield in the late 1940s and many of the landowners didn't want the unsightly electric poles on their property causing problems for the electric company. Telephones arrived in the late 1950s.

Some of the same families live in Craigfield today as did in the early years. They visit each other, they enjoy the quiet, and some who have visited other parts of the country find they are happiest in this peaceful, rural part of west Williamson County.

17

Cross Keys

Yellow Sandstone Home of Laban Hartley Jr. Still Prominent in Community

T HE CROSS KEYS COMMUNITY, nestled near Bethesda, was almost single-handedly settled by one man, Laban Hartley, and his family. Sources give Laban Hartley's birthplace as Snow Hill, Maryland, in 1742. He was of Scottish descent and, in 1778, enlisted in the Revolutionary War with a North Carolina company. During the Revolutionary War and until the Civil War, soldiers enlisted for a period of only three months. They would do a short tour of duty in the military, return home to help with the crops, then if they chose, re-enlist. They were not always assigned the same company. Laban Hartley enlisted in 1778, August 1779, and December 1779, 1780, and 1781. Despite all these efforts to perform a service to his country, Hartley still came out of the army a private. Hartley came to Williamson County on a land grant for service rendered in the war, but as a private, he was not entitled to as many acres as someone like one general, who was given 25,000 acres in Maury County. Laban Hartley Jr. preceded his father to Williamson County. Laban Jr. built a unique sandstone home in Cross Keys with yellow sandstone slabs so thick, it took four men to lift them into place. The home was built high off the ground in an effort to keep away the Indians and wild animals. The name "L. H. Hartley" was inscribed in the chimney.

The historic marker in front of the home gives the date of its construction as 1785, but a more likely date is 1821. The home remained in the Hartley family until about twenty years ago when it became property of the Dye family.

58

Laban Hartley and his wife Sarah had eight children, six daughters and two sons: Dennis, Jane, Nancy, Kate, Sarah, Abby, Patsy, and Laban Jr. He is the great-grandfather of many Cross Keys residents including the late Mrs. Carrie Trice. Laban Hartley's primary occupation was farming but he also made use of orchards planted near his home by making brandy for the tavern just across the road as well as a tavern in neighboring Maury County. Hartley lived to be 100 years old and died in 1842. His son Laban Jr. requested that one acre of land be set aside as a family burial ground, but strangely enough, Laban Sr. is not buried there. Instead he is buried in a plot on the south side of Flat Creek Road. Laban Hartley Jr. died in 1856 and in his will, bequeathed his favorite saddle horse and tack to one of his sons. His ten children were instructed to sell off all his remaining property and goods, except the family

The Choctaw Schoolhouse, the second one, is located on Choctaw Road and is now being used as a hay barn. The name came from the location of a cool spring nearby where Indians would camp. When the first school was torn down, the logs were dated as being approximately 128 years old. Some of the teachers at the Choctaw School were Miss Edna McIntosh, Miss Mary Daniels, Miss Irma Redfield, and Mrs. Tommy Anderson Gibbs. The second school was built on land given by Herbert McCall. When it closed, W. P. Scales was superintendent of schools.

burial grounds. This included his holdings in Maury County as well.

There seems to be some discrepancy as to how Cross Keys came to be named. It would seem logical that the Hartleys named it, but some say the Indians gave it the name. It was possibly called Cross Keys to identify the topographical features of the adjacent ridges. The most unusual is the legend of a man walking down the road looking for a community named Cross Keys. He came to that area in the county, let a set of keys in his possession fall to the ground and declared, "This must be Cross Keys!" Another suggestion is that it was named for a tavern whose sign was two crossed keys.

Nearby Mount Pisgah was an Indian burial ground and meeting place. At one time, the Choctaw Indians and white men in the area met to make peace and divide up the community. This was probably in the late 1700s or early 1800s. Besides the Hartley family, early settlers in the community included the Trice, Hargrove, Crafton, and Creswell families. The Trice family came to the area from Bedford County around 1880 and was one of the largest families in the community.

The community was never very large. There was never a post office, or gristmill, but there was a sorghum mill run by Edward Crafton on Choctaw Road, and there was also a funeral home in the community run by a Mr. Lavender. The store was first situated on Cross Keys Road under a shady black locust tree next to the home of James Trice. It was first owned and operated by Joe D. Trice. He started it around 1910 and sold it about twenty years later. Joe Trice opened a hardware store in Franklin in the present location of Sun Trust Bank on the town square. When he retired from that business, he went back to farming. Two other owners were Trav Wallace and a Mrs. Clendenon. The original store was torn down and a new one built across the road. Edward Crafton, who ran the sorghum mill, was known for the fact that he owned one of the first clocks in Cross Keys and people from all over would come by to see man's latest invention, sitting on the mantlepiece, in Crafton's home. It is still in existence and owned by a lady in Franklin.

Two churches serve the religious needs of the community. The Mount Zion United Methodist Church and the Cross Keys Baptist Church. The first Mount Zion Church was built of logs with four doors in the front and one on the side. It was located just above the present church building, which was constructed about 1910.

The Cross Keys Baptist Church was started in August 1954 by the King, Jackson, Smithson, and Newcomb families. It began as a tent meeting where worshipers decided they wanted a church of their own. The first place of worship was a storehouse, and the current building was constructed on land sold to the congregation by the Trice family.

The business of farming and caring for their families was uppermost in the minds of Cross Key folks, but one way the entire family had fun was at the pound suppers, where the ladies would make baskets of food and they were auctioned to the highest bidder by the pound. Several residents still live in the same homes they've had for years.

The present store, called Flippens Grocery, is about the only place of business. It's a quiet place to live and visit, with cats and dogs sunning themselves lazily in the summer sun on the porches, or hiding under a porch swing to get out of the heat. Laban Hartley would have been proud of his descendants in the Cross Keys area he started so long ago.

───── 18 ─────

Duplex

HOW THE COMMUNITY OF DUPLEX came by its name is a mystery. The dictionary defines the word "duplex" as a noun: a two-family house, divided vertically or horizontally, or, as an adjective: double, compound, having two parts. Neither definition seems to go with the community. In 1872, John Lee purchased a race horse named Duplex and the question is, did the community name come from the horse, or the horse's name come from the community? Duplex, the horse, was a beautiful mahogany bay pacer who set the record time of two minutes, seventeen seconds at a race track in Detroit, and his reputation was famous all over the nation. His portrait is still among the Lee family treasures.

Samuel Lee came into Williamson County around 1816, first building a log cabin and then the beautiful home, Maplewood, which was started around 1830 in the Duplex community. Furniture for Maplewood was purchased in New York and New Orleans, shipped by boat to Nashville, then transported by oxcart to Williamson County.

Two of Samuel's sons, John Lee and Samuel Lee Jr., served in the Civil War with the Tennessee Cavalry and mounted on horses from their homeplace, Maplewood. John fought in the Battle of Chickamauga, near Atlanta, and was in the escort accompanying Jefferson Davis from Richmond. John Lee surrendered at Washington, Georgia, in 1865, and returned home to Duplex to find a ruined plantation where the house had been used as a hospital, the fences burned, and the stock driven off the land. Another Lee home, Belle Lee Acres, was built for Samuel and John's sister Florence; and around these homes, the Duplex community grew. In addition to the Lees, early settlers included the McCord, Thompson, Stephens, Warner, Hartmon, Short, and Langley families.

A Revolutionary War soldier, Joshua Hadley was paying taxes in Williamson County as early as 1805 and living on land near Duplex as the result of a land grant. He is buried in Williamson County and it is said Andrew Jackson attended the funeral.

The first general store was started around 1870 and mail came to Duplex via the Pony Express system. Mail came from Spring Hill on a road started around 1816 by Samuel Lee.

The Mount Carmel Cumberland Presbyterian Church was the first Cumberland Presbyterian Church in Williamson County, and it was built on three and one-half acres of land deeded by Allen Bugg in 1827. The church was dedicated on October 27 of that year. The church was burned by Federal troops and was replaced with a building which stood until 1913, when it was lost to a windstorm. The present building was built in 1913. Community events centered around the church, events like ice cream suppers, taffy pulls, and lots of gospel singing.

Mount Carmel School, located next to the church, first went through the twelfth grade, and later only the eighth grade, with older students attending Bethesda. Teachers who taught at Mount Carmel School include Miss Vivian Grigsby, Miss Frances Hatcher, Miss Sallie Baugh, and tales are told of one teacher, a Mr. Walker, who was crippled, but didn't let that stop him. He let the children know who was boss. If they misbehaved, he would catch them around the neck with his cane.

Folks remember when Lewisburg Pike was a toll road and gypsies would camp near the bridge in the area. They would put on sideshows and no one knew exactly where they came from or where they went when they departed. Men living near county roads would donate five days of the year to repairing the roads. They did this with shovels and gravel as part of their county taxes.

After the first general store in 1870, Clint Thompson opened Thompson's Grocery on Lewisburg Pike around 1910. He would buy rabbits, chickens, eggs, and butter from area farmers and take them to market in Nashville, spending the night in Nashville and returning the next day with provisions for his store. He would also buy ice from the icehouse in Franklin and bring it back to a room behind the store where he would keep it cool by covering it with sawdust.

The post office was in the store, as it was in 1870, with a slot cut in the door for outgoing mail, and the incoming mail came from Spring Hill. It

Mount Carmel Cemetery.

didn't come from Franklin until 1967 and even then, the postman was not supposed to deliver it to Duplex; he would turn around at the Duplex Road and head back to Franklin. The late Jim Jefferson, a rural mail carrier for many years, managed to get through the government red tape to get the Duplex folks their mail, right in the community.

Clint Thompson was for many years a magistrate from the Duplex community. Thompson's Market is right next door to Clint's old store, where Clint once used an egg candling machine to see if the eggs he was taking to Nashville were good. If they had a dark spot on them, they were discarded. Charlie Moore ran the blacksmith shop behind the store, and there was a gristmill run by Jim Stephens as well as an undertaker's business nearby. Lundy Steele ran a sorghum mill behind the Duplex Church of God. Dairying is big business in Duplex, along with tobacco and corn. At one time, broom corn was grown and then made into brooms.

At the turn of the century, the doctors came from Bethesda. They were Dr. J. Blythe Core and Dr. William Clyde Eggleston. This was even before the Bethesda Road was built so they rode horseback across the fields, and old-timers remember, during cold winter nights, having to chop the ice off the doctor's feet in order to remove them from his stirrups.

Recreation, besides the gatherings at the church, came in the form of Thompson's Lake in the 1930s. James Thompson remembers helping dig the lake with pond scoops driven by mule power. It was on seven acres of land and used primarily for fishing and Fourth of July picnics. In the 1940s, big name entertainers like Bill Monroe and Roy Acuff would come to the picnic area to put on a show for the crowds. Later, there were also airplane rides for the more daring.

James Thompson tells about the day a remarkable feat was accomplished in Duplex. The men in the community managed to have a hog killing like none other; they killed 255 hogs in one day. They would clean them in the nearby creek, then cool them out on limestone rocks, and the men would sit up all night keeping the dogs away. One gargantuan hog weighed one thousand pounds and its head was even too heavy to carry to the creek for cleaning.

While Thompson's Market is the focal point of the community and many people have grown up and stayed in the area, some descendants of the Lee and Thompson families are in Franklin and other parts of the county. Duplex still has a warm feeling of community, and maybe someday, someone will learn how Duplex got its name.

19

Fairview

STARTED OUT AS "BARRENS"
LATER KNOWN AS "JINGO"

F AIRVIEW, IN WESTERN WILLIAMSON COUNTY, is more than just a community. It's the county's second incorporated town, incorporating in 1959. The community got its start when men traveled to the area claiming Revolutionary War land grants in the early 1800s. The soil in that part of the county proved too poor for farming and eventually, the earliest settlers drifted away. Later settlers came and cut down enormous amounts of trees, and possibly this is where the community's first name, Barrens, came from. Early in the twentieth century, a group of Jewish settlers came into the area, purchasing forty-acre lots, possibly on the Horn Tavern Road. One name people remember is Plotkin. Today only two homes remain which were owned by Jewish families and one is now used as a day care center on Highway 100.

The community has had three names over the years: Christiana was the first, followed by Jingo until the early 1930s, then finally, Fairview, a name given to the area by George Lampley. It was not named for the home called Fairview on Carter's Creek Pike.

The Fairview Church of Christ had its start as a brush arbor meeting in 1933, and within three months, the congregation had purchased its first building, a one-room schoolhouse. This served as the church building until 1942 when they built a basement church on Old Highway 96, but two years later it was sold to the county to be used as a lunch room for the Fairview Elementary School. The current building on Highway 100 was started in 1944 and has continued to grow with the community.

The Liberty Lincoln Church of Christ on Deer Ridge Road is one of the oldest in the community and was started when Will Lincoln, a casket maker, gave land for the building before the turn of the century. Methodist church circuit riders took care of the religious needs of several congregations, including the Greenbrier Church, Greens Chapel, Union Valley, Craigfield, and Pleasant Ridge.

Before the automobile, the wealthy of the area would arrive on Sunday mornings in their buggies, the others coming by wagon or horseback. Children's Day at one of the Methodist churches happened each year, when the children presented plays, sang songs, and everyone gathered for dinner on the ground. These, along with gospel meetings and community baseball games, gave a group of hard-working people some well-earned relaxation. There is a Primitive Baptist Church on Chester Road, and the Nazarenes, while they never had a church building, held tent meetings in Fairview.

Triangle School, on Westview Drive and now surrounded by weeds, overgrown bushes, and inhabited by stray cats, was an early consolidated school. In 1938, four schools—Aden, Liberty Hill, Naomi, and Hudgins—all pooled their resources and became the Triangle School. Fairview School came from the New Hope, Haskell, and Starkey Schools. School buses started when both schools were in use, but a few parents brought their children in cars and some walked or came by horse or mule. The current Fairview Elementary School came about with the consolidation of three of the larger west Williamson County schools, Triangle, New Hope, and Fairview.

The first school bus, which took older students to the Hillsboro High School, was purchased by Otto Green and S. E. Lehew. Parents were charged fifteen cents per day per child, and when the school bus broke down on the rough country roads, a flatbed truck was used to finish the trip to school. The first Fairview High School opened in 1956 and the elementary school in 1962. The current high school opened in 1981 and the old high school is used for a middle school.

The Fairview area was always closer to Dickson than Franklin because of the lack of a good road. Highway 100 helped somewhat when it was built in 1929. Before new Highway 96 was opened in the late 1960s, old 96 was in bad shape. Fairview folks said the best way to get to Franklin was to head north on Highway 100, then south on Hillsboro Road, the long way around. Highway 100 was started in 1929 and paved in 1930. Men doing the construction work lived in tents, and the horses and mules used to do the heavy work were stabled in Will Daugherty's barn. Men building the road were paid five dollars per day, and the road was cut through to Jackson, Tennessee.

The first business, Daugherty's Store, run by W. F. (Will) Daugherty was started in 1922. Will and his wife were parents of thirteen children, and they all helped with the family business. Supplies to trade were taken to Nashville by covered wagon. It was a three-day trip, leaving on Monday and returning on Wednesday. Besides the usual chickens and eggs, the Daugherty's would send possum hides, rabbit, quail, country ham, cream, and butter. They would return with overalls, sheets, bolts of cloth, sugar, coffee, nails, horseshoes and trace chains for the mules, as well as plow points for the farm equipment.

Other stores were run by Kern Givens, Lee Lampley, and M. T. Taylor. Taylor was father of Tom Taylor, who still has a general merchandise store on Highway 100, and was the first mayor of Fairview in 1959. Besides grocery stores, there were peddling trucks which took staples to the folks way back in the country, and one of these routes was run by Andrew Gardner. Ed Southern ran a gristmill on Southern Road, and there were three or four mills in the community for corn, wheat flour, sorghum, and the area was also dotted with sawmills.

Before it became Fairview, the community was called Jingo. Some say the name came from the slang expression "Well, by jingo." Jingo was the name of the post office, about three miles from the present town. One of the postmasters was Johnny Griffen and most of the mail was carried by horseback. At one time there may have been other post offices between Jingo and the present Fairview, at Aden and Naomi. When Highway 100 came through, the post office was moved closer to the highway, and about 1933, the name was changed to Fairview.

Hudgins' Cemetery is unique in that Mr. Hudgins gave land to anyone who wanted to be buried there, at no charge. When a member of the community passed away, someone would go by horseback to tell the others. People would stop whatever they were doing, come to the house and help the family, or go to the cemetery to prepare the burial ground. Hay would be put on a wagon frame or truck to keep the body from jostling on the way to its final resting place. Will Daugherty had to take his mother to be buried in this manner.

In the 1920s, a typhoid fever epidemic went through the community. One of the early doctors was a Dr. Spencer who came all the way from White Bluff. He would be brought to the area by a man on horseback and even though he was driving a Ford Model T, the rough back country road

Hudgins' Cemetery.

made travel difficult, and often the horseback rider had to stop to let the car catch up to him.

The first automobile in Fairview, a Star car, was owned by J. J. Richardson. There was only one brand of gasoline available, Standard Oil, and that could be purchased at Daugherty's Store. Johnson was a member of a pickin' and singin' group during the 1930s. He played the banjo, along with Rufus Hall and Leonard Parker on the fiddles. Mostly they played for the enjoyment of their family and friends. John Bethshears had the first radio, and telephones brought communications to the area in the 1950s.

Fairview was incorporated and made a municipality in August 1959. It is run by a commission, with one of the commissioners becoming the mayor. Tom Taylor was the first mayor and the community had the distinction of having one of the first women mayors when Mrs. Mary Clinard took over the job in the late 1960s. When campaigning for Fairview's first mayor, Tom Taylor ran on the issue of bringing city water to the community. City water came to Fairview in the mid-1960s. The police department with Shorty Mangrum as the first chief of police was started in 1971, and one of the first of many industries was the Fairview Casting Company.

Fairview has come a long way from the time of Horn Springs Tavern where whiskey could be bought for a dime a quart. The tavern was given the name because Noah Harrison, tavern owner, cut off the tip end of a cow horn, plugged it with a stopper and used it for a draw glass. The tavern was also used as a post office. Some early postmasters from 1841 to 1849 were Isaac Twomey, George Harris, and James A. Cunningham.

Many names are familiar in the Fairview area and have been there for years such as Daugherty, Sullivan, Stinson, Lampley, Bethshears, and Mangrum. The town continues to grow and thrive, with a health clinic, a senior citizens' center, and it was honored by several visits from then Governor Lamar Alexander.

The determination of the Fairview community is demonstrated in the acquisition of a library. The Fairview Home Demonstration Club started keeping a couple of shelves filled with books from the Williamson County Public Library back in the 1960s. The first real home for the library was a trailer which the city commission purchased for one dollar, reworked, and gave to the library as a permanent home in June 1980. It is located next to the city hall on Highway 100 and is a branch of the county library. Any book can be ordered through the interlibrary system.

The city of Fairview is working to meet the needs of the residents, and because it is located close to Interstate 40 on the west for easy access to Nashville and has Highway 96 connecting it to Franklin, more new residents join the lifelong residents in western Williamson County every year.

─────20─────

Fernvale

AREA FAMOUS FOR ITS LUSH FERNS
AND SULPHUR SPRINGS

THE COMMUNITY OF FERNVALE, located west of Franklin off Old Harding Road, was once a resort community, with the well-to-do from Nashville and Franklin traveling by train and buggy to take advantage of the sulphur spring waters. They came to get away from the oppressive summer heat of the city, meet friends, and enjoy hunting and fishing for trout in nearby creeks, or relax with card games on the wide veranda of the hotel. Fernvale Springs was originally called Smith Springs, after the first owner Samuel Smith. Smith, the descendant of an Englishman, came to Nashville in 1812. In 1822 he and his family moved to the South Harpeth area near Fernvale and prospered there. At his death in 1838, he left his wife and nine children with an estate worth more than ten thousand dollars. After the Civil War, a prominent Franklin attorney John B. McEwen bought the springs from the Smith descendants, and developed Smith Springs into a popular resort area. It was his wife's niece who gave it the name Fernvale for all the lush green foliage growing in the area. Log cabins were built on the hillside for families, and a large two-story hotel was built on both sides of the road, with a connecting passageway under which traffic could pass. There were thirty-two white columns and porches both upstairs and down.

Fernvale was advertised in glowing terms and had numerous conveniences for the early part of the 1900s. There was a free, direct line furnished by the Cumberland Telephone Company connecting with Western Union in Franklin. A man could bring his family by horse and carriage, or hacks were supplied at the train depots of Bellevue and Franklin. The trip was

71

about two hours. Mail was delivered daily, and besides hunting and fishing, there was bowling, tennis, and dancing to music by Professor De Piere of Nashville. No gambling or drinking intoxicating beverages was allowed. Cost was modest: two dollars a day, thirty dollars a month, and servants and children stayed for half-price.

People came from Middle Tennessee and as far away as Montgomery, Alabama, to take advantage of the sulphur spring water. Colonel McEwen developed two additional springs besides the one that had been in operation for many years. The springs were advertised as a remedy for many ills, including dyspepsia, kidney ailments, nerves, and rheumatism, and the water was even recommended for teething children during their second summer. In 1901, Robert McEwen was hotel manager, and an advertisement of the day claimed the resort was a "park of ten acres, with fountains, icehouse (125 tons of ice), bathhouse, gardens with fresh vegetables, a laundry, hack service, and a store," and the hotel boasted 114 rooms. In 1905, the McEwen family sold the resort to William Pepper Bruce. As a child, Bruce had come with his family to the springs, when it was known as Smith Springs, and as an adult, he purchased the hotel, springs, and over 3500 acres of land. It was in operation for several more years, and in 1910, the hotel burned and all that remains are the Mayfield Springs, which can be seen from the road, and the white latticework gazebo-like structure which covers the springs. There is a sign, which was constructed by the Fernvale Home Demonstration Club in 1960 which reads, "Those of you who were here, now are old and few. Should you return for a bit of cheer, we surely welcome you."

Another industry which contributed to Williamson County history was the Caney Fork Furnace, located near the Caney Fork Creek in the Fernvale area. It may have been one of the many furnaces owned by Cheatham County ironmaster Montgomery Bell. Ironmaking was once a highly successful and lucrative business in Middle Tennessee, and the Caney Fork Furnace was in operation from the early 1800s until after the Civil War. In fact, cannon balls from Caney Fork were carried by oxcart to the Cumberland River in Nashville where they were shipped by barge to troops with General Andrew Jackson in New Orleans in 1815. In 1857, iron was processed in the furnace to make the pillars of the front portico of the Williamson County Courthouse. The columns were cast in a foundry which stood a few yards north of the Lillie Mill. During the time of the Civil War, minié and cannon balls were produced at Caney Fork, right next to the running waters of the Caney Fork Creek.

One of the early churches in the area was the South Harpeth Church of Christ started in 1806 in a community once called Linton. Earliest settlers

Church of Christ building.

who came to the community settled in specific areas decided by their wealth. The rich people were entitled to the bottomland, while the less fortunate settled in the hills and hollows near the Natchez Trace.

Jeremiah Kirby made guns at Fernvale before he moved to Texas around 1870. One of his blacksmith shops was burned by the Yankees when he refused to repair their guns. Today, Kirby guns are collectors' items.

Among the early settlers were the Allison, Linton, Knight, Smith, and King families. The Linton family came from North Carolina where Silas Linton, son of the original settler, Hezekiah, operated a store and gristmill, and was owner of 1000 acres of land.

The gentlemen who owned thousands of acres of land, the iron furnace, and the once-thriving resort of Fernvale are an indelible part of the history of Williamson County. It's a reminder of a time, not too long ago, when the gentlefolk would travel to the quiet countryside to relax with the waters, and a reminder that an industry like the Caney Fork Furnace may have vanished, but the pillars on the courthouse are strong and sturdy reminders of the past.

21

Flagpole

SITE OF SUMMERTIME
TENT MEETING

THE COMMUNITY OF FLAGPOLE won't be found on the newest map of Williamson County; actually, one would be hard pressed to find it on any map of the last thirty years, but it exists. While Flagpole never had stores, schools or churches in the community itself, it was known for a huge tent meeting which took place every year in August.

Flagpole is located just off Pinewood Road near Walker Hill Road. It was christened "Flagpole" because there were several large trees in the middle of the property. Men in the area cut the boughs from one particularly tall tree, leaving one bough running straight up. They then fastened a United States flag to a pole, attached the pole to the tree, and set the flag waving high in the air. During World War II, a tall steel tower, 120 feet high, was erected on the Flagpole acreage, from the top of which you could see into five counties: Williamson, Maury, Dickson, Davidson, and Hickman.

The tent meeting at Flagpole was a major event in the western portion of the county. It took place every year during the first two weeks in August until around 1918. People would come by wagon, horse and buggy, and all matter of conveyance from as far away as Kentucky and Alabama to attend the non-denominational service. The men would haul sawdust and lumber from nearby sawmills to create a temporary floor for the tent and make wooden benches for the worshipers. Children would sit on the floor if there wasn't room to sit with their families. The services lasted all day, concluding by nightfall. Families would camp at the meeting place, each bringing their own provisions for the two-week stay. They would eat in family units rather than

Barn at Flagpole.

together as we do today with the popular dinner-on-the-ground method of sharing our meals. Water was brought in daily by horse-drawn wagon by Reuben Anglin in three large barrels. By 1918, the Greenbrier Methodist Church had been built, one of the first in the area. Also, the coming of the automobile made transportation to larger communities more accessible.

The five acres which made up Flagpole were later sold by Meacham to Tom Mays, who sold it to Clayton Dugan. Today the land is owned by Joe Moss. Families in the Flagpole area included the Anglins, Sullivans, Stinsons, and Walkers. At the turn of the century, children went to the Post Oak School through the eighth grade, and provisions were purchased at J. C. Green's store. The store building itself is still standing on Oscar Green's property, on the corner of Shoals Branch and Pinewood Roads. Today, Sullivan's Store is just past Walker Hill Road and one can still buy everything from toothpicks to horse collars.

Timber and sawmills were the prime industry in the western part of Williamson County. At one time farmers also had sheep as well as hogs and cattle. Progress does bring good things to an area, but it would be nice if the name Flagpole was on the Williamson County maps.

22

Flat Creek

EDWARDS GROVE CHURCH, STARTED IN 1833, STILL IN USE TODAY

F LAT CREEK, IN THE SOUTHEASTERN PART OF THE COUNTY, takes its name from the creek in the area. Four Revolutionary War soldiers from the same family were among the earliest settlers. David, Thomas, John, and Isaac Gillespie all received land grants in the early 1800s. Thomas Gillespie was given a grant of 4000 acres but he never used the grant and his land was sold. Isaac Gillespie settled on 600 acres near Flat Creek. This same Isaac gave land for the Edwards Grove Church in 1833 and the church is still in existence today. In April 1813, Isaac's brother David was an overseer in charge of cleaning and keeping in good repair the main road from Maury County to Nashville. In old records, some portion of the land was called Flat Woods, and David Gillespie gave his land to be used as a church, with church members having permission to use his nearby spring.

Colonel Hardee Murfree at one time owned a 6000-acre grant on the headquarters of Flat Creek when it was still Indian territory. Another early family was the Pollack family. They soon changed their name to Polk. Jane Gillespie, granddaughter of Thomas and Naomi Gillespie, was the mother of James K. Polk, eleventh president of the United States.

Most Revolutionary soldiers who came from North Carolina were given land grants in this area. However, at the time of the Revolutionary War, all of this was North Carolina. In fact, this area was called Davidson County for General Davidson who had been killed by the British. One document states that an Alexander family settled in the Flat Creek area around 1790 and this was Indian Territory. In the Flat Creek area, there are more Revolutionary War soldiers buried in the Steele Cemetery than anywhere else in the county. This is also the burial site of Laban Hartley, founder of the Cross Keys community just up the road.

There are four slave cemeteries in the area, one of which became the foundation for an interesting occurrence in 1906. Before that year, Mayhew Smithson had built a barn on the property where one of the slave cemeteries was located. He did not like the cemetery there, so he dug up the sandstone markers, and laid them around his barn. One June day in 1906, he wanted to get the wheat thrashed and the straw in the barn. It was a Sunday afternoon, and he asked his hired hands to help. They were not eager to be of assistance, as it was a Sunday, and also they did not like working with the remnants of the slave cemetery around the barn where the straw was to be stored. According to one eyewitness, during the course of the afternoon, a large thundercloud came up overhead, and a sudden bolt of lightning came out of the sky, striking the barn and setting it on fire. Coincidence? Maybe, but Mayhew Smithson promised he would rebuild the barn on the same site, and his barn built in 1907 is still standing.

A schoolhouse was built in 1905 when five acres of land was purchased and a two-room schoolhouse built. It was used as a school until the 1940s when it became the local community club. Records show as many as three blacksmith shops in Flat Creek. One was run by Jim Meeks, probably the earliest, another by G. R. Tucker around 1878, and a Mr. Jordan and a Mr. Engel ran the third blacksmith shop. Flat Creek could also boast of a fraternity called "Woodsmen of the World," with a meeting place over an early general store. At one time, there was also a race track around Flat Creek.

One church, started in 1833 and still going on today, was the Edwards Grove Church. Isaac Gillespie gave the land for the first church, a log structure. Forty years later, September 1873, James Edwards and his wife Hannah gave the church two acres of land where the present building stands. They were members of the Methodist Episcopal Church until 1977 when the congregation voted to become independent.

This area was also the location of the county poorhouse, when in 1829, Andrew Andrews sold the county forty acres of land for $350 for the benefit of the poor. The county then bought twenty more acres, and agreed to pay Mark Andrews $250 to build the ﾠ　ﾠ　re to be used as the poorhouse.

W. L. (Tip) Pate built a home just across from the Baptist meeting grounds, and called it Baptist Rest. The home sat on 400 acres of land and is listed on the county map of 1878. The home burned in 1923.

The first Reed's store was started by Jerome B. Reed while he was still a teenager, in the 1860s. Its location was in the home of his grandfather Tucker, as Reed was an orphan and living with the Tuckers. The Reed family owned the store for many years, and one can still see the mail slot under the door. When Reed's store officially closed, Wiley White opened a large general store on Flat Creek Road.

World War I, around 1917, was the time telephones were in use. They were Farmer Exchange phones. Farmers who had telephones owned and maintained their own phones, and their phone lines connected them to the main office, or "central," in this case, College Grove.

In addition to names like Wallace, and Gillespie, early settlers in Flat Creek include the Lester, Sanford, Woods, Owen, Reynolds, Reed, Corlette, Hazelwood, Chrisman, Wall, Allison, and Mincey families. Families who have lived in the quiet community of Flat Creek for many generations say it's a good community where people may not see each other for weeks, but if an emergency arises, they're there. It's a family community, without the rough elements. They're able to change with the times yet keep enough of the past to keep a proper perspective on life today.

—23—

Forest Home

FOREST HOME, LOCATED OFF OLD HILLSBORO ROAD, is an area full of beautifully preserved old homes, rock walls, and split-rail fences. A stone bridge in the area once carried Andrew and Rachel Jackson on their travels and it also felt the hoofbeats of horses carrying Andrew Jackson and his men to fight the Battle of New Orleans. Historic memorabilia in a private collection include the pistols used to capture Aaron Burr on his flight from the U.S. government.

While Forest Home was never a major community, it was an area of wealthy landowners, with descendants of these first families still very prominent in the community. Homes with names like Montpier, Meeting of the Waters, Old Town, Walnut Hill, Two Rivers, and River Grange, names which evoke memories of a gentler time along the Harpeth River, still grace the countryside near Forest Home.

Old Town is the name of the home built by Thomas Brown on the Natchez Trace Road. The bridge at Old Town was built in 1801 when the secretary of war ordered the Natchez Trace be widened for the passage of mail, and it would later carry the troops down to New Orleans. The bridge was in use for 112 years, until 1913, and the stones are in disrepair today.

Meeting of the Waters, the oldest Perkins' home, was built by Thomas Hardin Perkins soon after he arrived in Williamson County, around 1800. At that time, the area was such a wilderness the house was probably built with a brick in one hand, and a gun for protection from the Indians in the other. The name came from the home's proximity to the junction of the Big

Meeting of the Waters.

Harpeth and the West Harpeth Rivers. This beautiful home saw much activity over the years. During the Civil War, it was the site of a confrontation when drunken Federal troops began looting livestock, household items, and the children's possessions, with the youngsters watching them from the upstairs windows.

Nicholas Perkins, a relative of Thomas Hardin Perkins, came to this county in the early 1800s, but prior to that was putting his name in the history books for a deed which occurred in Mississippi. In 1807, Perkins was register in a Mississippi land office, when, working late the night of February 18, 1807, he heard the sound of approaching horses. Looking outside, he recognized one rider as the former vice president, Aaron Burr, who, three years earlier, had killed Alexander Hamilton in a duel. In 1807, he was wanted by the government for treason and was fleeing south. Perkins helped to apprehend the man, and the next day was put in charge of taking Burr back to the Federal authorities in Washington. At one point, Burr tried to escape, whereupon Nicholas Perkins drew his pistols but did not use them. Burr stood trial in the nation's capital but was not convicted. The pistols used by Perkins are still in the possession of his descendants in this county.

In 1808, Nicholas Perkins came to Williamson County and married his cousin Mary, who lived at Meeting of the Waters. By 1810 he owned 12,000 acres of land in the Forest Home area. He also had the dubious distinction of introducing Johnson grass into the county. Nicholas Perkins built his home, Montpier, about 1821. This was the third of the Perkins' homes to be built. The second was Two Rivers, the home of Nicholas Tate Perkins, a relative of Nicholas and Thomas. Nicholas Perkins called himself "Bigbee" to distinguish himself from the other Nicholas in the family. He came by this name because at one time he owned land on the Tombigbee River.

Two Rivers was built in 1802 and was originally called Poplar Grove. The home was sold in 1848 to the parents of Colonel William M. Shy, a Civil War colonel who died in the Battle of Nashville. Shy's name was in the news in 1978 when vandals desecrated his grave at Two Rivers; he was reburied at the same sight with full honors. His original metal casket is now in the Carter House Museum. When a storm went through the area in 1927, many beautiful poplar trees were lost on the grounds, and the name changed to Two Rivers denoting the West and Big Harpeth Rivers around the estate.

River Grange was built by Nicholas Tate Perkins for his daughter Mary and her husband. It was originally called Locust Valley, but was renamed River Grange by Episcopal Bishop Charles Quintard because it was a wheat farm and encircled by the Harpeth River.

Another home of Nicholas "Bigbee" Perkins was given to his daughter Sara and was called Walnut Hill. The home was the site of a landmark state supreme court decision when, in 1850, the court reversed a lower-court decision in the case of a slave administering poison to a five-week-old baby. The supreme court found for the slave over the master. Walnut Hill was built about 1840 and sold many times between 1867 and 1958. In 1958 it was purchased by Mr. and Mrs. Claude Callicott. The second floor of the home had been completely blown off a tornado in the early 1900s but the Callicotts were able to restore the entire house to its former glory and renamed it Eventide. It was sold in 1995.

After 1900, the community boasted two general stores on Hillsboro Road, one across from the other. One was run by Robert McPherson, the other by a Mr. King. Voting during the summer primary elections took place outside under the shade trees. The November elections took place in the warmth of a store. The tollgate for Hillsboro Road was located near Barrell Springs Hollow Road and was mentioned on the 1878 map of the county. Walter Roberts, longtime resident of the area, once lived in the toll-house, and he remembered people paying toll even after the road was no longer a toll road.

One early church was the Locust Valley Church, on River Grange property. It later became Moores Chapel and burned in 1890. The present Forest Hills Church of Christ was started in 1950 by the Lindsley Avenue Church of Christ, using students from David Lipscomb College for preachers. The church started in what once was Forest Hill School. Teachers at the one-teacher school would board at the house across the road. Mrs. Mattie Logan Payne was an early teacher along with Miss Bertha Moore. There was also a school for black children, called Perkins School, on land donated by the Perkins family.

A blacksmith shop and a distillery were also part of the community. One day, someone forgot to put a plug in one of the kegs, and the liquor ran out across Old Hillsboro Road, with neighbors coming to enjoy free samples.

Early family names besides Perkins include Payne, Bateman, Hassell, Smith, Stone, Bradley, and Brown. Years of history have accumulated in the Perkins' homes, and as long as these magnificent dwellings remain in the hands of families who care about them and remember the past while enjoying the present, Forest Home will continue to be a place we can look to with pride.

24

Franklin

COUNTY SEAT NAMED FOR
BENJAMIN FRANKLIN

F RANKLIN, THE COUNTY SEAT OF WILLIAMSON COUNTY, was created by act of the Tennessee Legislature on October 26, 1799, and the town laid out on land belonging to Abram Maury. Named for Benjamin Franklin, the county held its first court on February 3, 1800, in Thomas McKay's tavern. Such were the beginnings of a town which was to become the site of one of the bloodiest battles in the Civil War, home of a world champion Tennessee Walking horse, the first three-story building in the state, many historic and elegant homes, and a fifteen-block downtown area which is listed in the National Register of Historic Places.

The first home in Franklin was built by Ewin Cameron in 1798 on Second Avenue, where the parking lot for City Hall Mall is today. By 1835, the population had grown to 1500 people with five schools, four churches, three clergymen, eight doctors, seven lawyers, and a number of blacksmith shops, hatters, saddlers, wagoners, and a gunsmith.

The Williamson County Courthouse, constructed in 1859, is the third courthouse. The first, a log structure built in 1800, and the second, built in 1809, was a brick building in the middle of the town square. Franklin's first inn was located behind what is now the Old, Old Jail on Bridge Street. It was built by Benjamin White in 1803 and was visited by famous gentlemen like Andrew Jackson, Thomas Hart Benton, and Felix Grundy. A small brick building on East Main Street, now the Visitors' Information Center for the Franklin-Williamson County Heritage Foundation, was built around 1813 and keeps its place in history as the location of the first successful use of anesthetic in the Middle Tennessee area. It was administered by Dr. Daniel

McPhail to treat a man with gunshot wounds.

The number of elegant, well-preserved homes in the Franklin city limits are a tribute to their owners down through the years and to organizations like the Heritage Foundation who oversee the preservation of a way of life from the past that can continue into generations of the future. One of the earliest homes, still in beautifully preserved condition, is the Marshall house on Third Avenue. The home was built around 1805 and was owned for many years by John Marshall, prominent Franklin attorney. It was also the home of Park Marshall, author of *The History of Franklin*, and mayor of both Franklin and Nashville.

The Moran house, just behind the Williamson County Courthouse, was built in 1820 by Charles Moran, an accomplished cabinetmaker, who made furniture for Andrew Jackson's home, The Hermitage. The house was later purchased by Dr. Thomas Pope in 1896, where he practiced dentistry in the office next to his home until his death in 1947. He was the father of Miss Mary Pope, who resided in her homeplace for many years, teaching Franklin young people the joys of classical music on the piano. Miss Mary was well known for her work in the Presbyterian church and active in the Allied Arts Club. She is also remembered for the number of cats kept in her home.

The Eaton home, an elegant residence in the Federal style, was built in 1818 and was once the home of Elizabeth Eaton, mother of John Henry Eaton, a member of Andrew Jackson's presidential cabinet. When Jackson was elected president, he appointed Eaton as his secretary of war causing a furor which split Jackson's cabinet. The commotion was over the marriage of Eaton to Margaret O'Neill, a recently widowed daughter of a Washington innkeeper not accepted by Washington society. Eaton later resigned his post and was appointed governor of the Territory of Florida.

Most of the early homes in Franklin were built as two-story structures. A beautiful landmark home on the corner of Third Avenue and Margin Street, built by John Miller in 1866, is only one-story high. This was because his wife was afraid of thunderstorms. The home, which now houses the O'More College of Design on South Margin Street, was called Winstead Place and was built by William O'Neal Perkins in 1866, reflecting more the Victorian era than the antebellum style of earlier times.

Splendored, home of former mayor of Franklin, Dr. Jeff Bethurum, was built on Franklin Road in 1902 and is important in the history of Franklin because it was the scene of a number of "firsts." It was the first home to have a waterworks system powered by a gasoline engine which pumped water from a nearby spring to a tank and then was piped into the house. It was also the first to have a complete Delco lighting system. Another first was central heat supplied from a furnace in the basement.

One Franklin home has gained importance for its part in American history. The Carter house, built around 1830 by Fountain Branch Carter, was the scene of several skirmishes during the Civil War and on November 30, 1864, was right in the middle of the Battle of Franklin. In 1951 the Carter House Association was formed to see to the restoration of the home, and in 1961 it was placed on the Register of Historic Landmarks. The Carter House Museum on the grounds behind the house was dedicated in 1982 to house Civil War memorabilia.

Many religious denominations are represented by the various churches in Franklin, one of the earliest being First United Methodist Church. In 1798 Abram Maury set aside one of his own lots for a Methodist Meeting House on what is now First Avenue. A second church was constructed for the congregation in 1826 on what is now Second Avenue. The present building, on the west side of Fifth Avenue was built in 1871 and has been in continuous use, growing with the needs of the congregation.

The mother church of the Episcopal Diocese of Tennessee is St. Paul's Episcopal Church on West Main Street. The church was formally organized in 1827 and met at the Masonic Hall under the leadership of James Hervey Otey. Otey was elected bishop of Tennessee in 1833, but stayed on as rector of St. Paul's until 1835. The church building itself was completed in 1834 and like so many buildings in town, was used as a hospital during the Battle of Franklin. There are still marks on the pillars where it is said troops tried to chop them up for use as firewood. Early in the century, Tiffany stained glass windows were installed and youngsters can actually feel the folds in the robes of the angel in one window.

The First Presbyterian Church was organized by Gideon Blackburn in 1811, and in 1815 a small brick church was built on Indigo Street (now Fourth Avenue). The present site, on Main Street and Fifth Avenue, was purchased in 1841, and the current church building is the third one on that site. The first was severely damaged by Federal troops during the war and the second destroyed by fire.

The Fourth Avenue Church of Christ building grew out of a visit to Franklin in 1851 by Alexander Campbell, an evangelist who wished to restore New Testament Christianity. But two local preachers, Andrew Craig and Joel Anderson, had been preaching Campbell's doctrine since 1833, and a lot for a church building had been bought from Thomas Hardin Perkins Sr. on Fourth Avenue. When Campbell came to Franklin in 1851, over four hundred people responded and the first building on Fourth Avenue was constructed in 1852. The church, which first started out with seventeen members, now has a membership of over a thousand and is housed in a new structure still on Fourth Avenue, completed in 1977.

The oldest and most unique religious structure in Franklin is the Masonic Hall on Second Avenue. The hall was finished in 1823 and was the first three-story building in the state. It was here in 1830 that President Andrew Jackson, John H. Eaton, and John Coffee met with a delegation of Chickasaw Indian chiefs dressed in full regalia, to discuss the sale of their lands. This was to eventually lead to the tribes removal to Oklahoma and the Trail of Tears. During the Civil War, Confederate soldiers used the roof of the hall to see what was happening at Fort Granger, the Federal fort just north of town.

Two fascinating documents, now in the possession of Margaret Henderson Gentry MacPherson of Franklin, are the diaries of her great-grandfather, Dr. Samuel Henderson Sr., whose recollections date from 1834 until 1876. The other diary is that of John H. Henderson, her grandfather and father of the late Judge John H. Henderson Jr. The reminiscences of Dr. Samuel Henderson cover daily events such as the weather, the crops planted, and the deaths of famous men like Andrew Jackson and prominent local people like Nicholas Perkins. Henderson aided in the burial of Perkins in the Masonic order. Henderson also recorded several cholera epidemics in 1849 and again in 1873. In May 1852 he recorded the beginning of surveying for the Franklin-Lewisburg Turnpike and indicated he was responsible for building a portion of the road which passed his property. The record of April 11, 1862, is indicative of the importance of events. He writes: "Began to plant corn. Upwards of forty thousand Federal soldiers have passed through Franklin."

The diary was carried on by his son John H. Henderson, from 1882 until 1913. This diary indicates there was a business called the Franklin Sugar and Syrup Mills which was started August 30, 1884. However, the business did not generate enough funds to keep going and even though Henderson had invested $500 in it, it closed in two months, but the problems were not completely settled until four years later. His records also indicate that city hall burned on Christmas Day 1887, but he managed to save information from his law office. In September 1888, he took note of the fact there was a yellow fever epidemic in town and Franklin was put under quarantine, as were most of the towns along the railroad. In November 1899, the Confederate Monument was dedicated and John H. Henderson, after having worked fourteen years to make the monument a reality, was responsible for the inscription on one side of the base: "We who saw and knew them well, are witness to the coming ages of their fidelity."

Franklin was the site of numerous private schools, such as Harpeth Academy, the Franklin Female Institute, the Tennessee Female College, and Battle Ground Academy. The first Harpeth Academy chartered in 1806 was located on Del Rio Pike. Presbyterian minister Gideon Blackburn was the headmaster in 1811. A later leader was Episcopal Bishop of Tennessee James Otey. One famous pupil, Matthew Fontaine Maury, went on to become known as the Pathfinder of the Seas. In the early years of the Civil War, the school was burned by a Federal detachment, and the bricks and stones were used in the construction of Fort Granger. Fifty years later, the government paid the school four thousand dollars to be used for educational purposes. A new Harpeth Academy started on Franklin Road in 1969.

The Tennessee Female College was begun in 1857 with John Marshall as president of the board of trustees. The school was located near Fifth and Margin Streets, and educated the daughters of Franklin's leading citizens. During the Federal occupation of the town, the school was used as a Union hospital, and after the war, classes resumed in 1865. The building burned in 1886; a new, three-story brick structure replaced it. The enrollment gradually diminished with the coming of public schools, and the building was torn down in 1916 to make way for more modern structures.

The Franklin Female Institute was housed in a brick building at Five Points. The school started in 1847 in a small house, under the direction of Rev. A. N. Cunningham, a Presbyterian minister. Girls at the school watched Federal and Confederate soldiers pass under the windows of the school before the Battle of Franklin, and on the day of battle, were sent home early. Following the war, both boys and girls attended the school until the building was torn down in 1905.

The next school on this site in 1907 was the Franklin Grammar School. Franklin High School started on the second floor of the grammar school in 1910, and in 1926 classes moved to a building on Columbia Avenue. The high school burned in 1956 and the grammar school burned in 1962. Today, students attend elementary school at seven locations: Franklin Elementary School on Fairground Street; Franklin Middle School on 96 West; Freedom Intermediate School on Glass; Johnson Elementary School on Mount Hope Street; Liberty School on Liberty Pike; and Moore School on Lewisburg Pike. Grades seven through nine attend the Franklin Junior High School on Mount Hope Street.

Battle Ground Academy (BGA) was first known as the Mooney School, after its first headmaster W. D. Mooney, and was situated then, as today, on the scene of some of the bloodiest fighting of the Battle of Franklin. The original building burned in 1902 and students attended classes at the Everbright mansion just across the street. A new building was constructed, but it too burned in 1905, and classes again were held at Everbright until another building was constructed. The school flourished under the administration of George I. Briggs, from 1925 until 1944. The annual Tug of War between the school's two societies, the Greers and the Platos, began in 1935. For a number of years, BGA was a boarding school and day school only for boys. However, in recent years, girls have been admitted, and it is no longer a boarding school.

The Civil War wrought many changes in the town of Franklin. The area had been under Federal occupation for four years with troops stationed at Fort Granger just across the Harpeth River. Then on November 30, 1864, one of the bloodiest battles to occur in the war took place in Franklin, when Confederate General John Bell Hood met Union General John Schofield in fighting around Columbia Pike. Six thousand Confederate soldiers were left dead and over two thousand Union soldiers were lost to the battle. Four slain generals, Cleburne, Granbury, Strahl, and Adams, were laid on the porch of the McGavock home, Carnton. General Gist died on Boyd Mill Pike, and General Carter died ten days later. The Confederate Cemetery, just outside Franklin off Lewisburg Pike, is on land given by Colonel John McGavock to give southern soldiers a more protected final resting place. Money was raised by Franklin citizens and relatives from other southern states. The Confederate monument, one of Franklin's most familiar and popular sites, was dedicated November 30, 1899, with much ceremony. The monument had been constructed with children's pennies and the hard-earned money of Confederate veterans and their families, and spearheaded by the Franklin Chapter Fourteen of the Daughters of the Confederacy. It was a small way of remembering those young men who had shown such courage some thirty years before. Several weeks before the statue was unveiled, while it was being raised into place, a horse and buggy became tangled in one of the supporting ropes, and a piece of the hat was broken off. It remains that way today.

The Williamson County Bank and Trust Company began in 1889 on the town square under its first president J. W. Harrison. Today, as Nation's Bank, it is one of the county's largest financial institutions with several branch offices.

A Franklin cemetery.

For over 100 years after the Civil War, Franklin and its surroundings continued the same year after year. This was a farming community, with Main Street stores doing a brisk business on Saturday nights, and the economy based on the main cash crop, tobacco. The annual Rotary Club Rodeo, which has grown to become the largest rodeo east of the Mississippi, started in 1949 and has become a Franklin tradition. With the coming of Interstate 65 and subdivisions in the 1960s, things began to change in a hurry, and Williamson County became the fastest-growing county in the state. Shopping centers sprang up on the east side of town, near the interstate, and north on Hillsboro Road.

The Williamson County Hospital, serving the medical needs of the community since 1958, was replaced by the Williamson County Medical Center. The new facility on Curd Lane brings, more modern medical facilities to the mid-state area. The Mack Hatcher Memorial Parkway, opened December 1985, connects Columbia Pike with Hillsboro Road, coming out just past the Franklin High School.

Franklin and Williamson County residents lived through the devastation of a bloody Civil War battle which completely erased a way of life, and Middle Tennesseans can withstand the changes coming in the future. They have always enjoyed a rich heritage and a gentle way of life with friends and neighbors. The years ahead may prove to be exciting; Franklin can only wait and see.

Franklin Armistice Day Parade, 1934. Gilbert Sullivan, Salmon Thornton, Claude Reese.

25

Grassland

COMMUNITY GREW AROUND LOG HOME ON HILLSBORO ROAD

THE GRASSLAND COMMUNITY, located on Hillsboro Road between Franklin and Brentwood, is one of the county's fastest growing areas. The Grassland community began growing around what started as a log home on Hillsboro Road, built in 1802, and now serves as the clubhouse for the River Rest Condominiums. The home was built by William Leaton II and was originally two log rooms and a dog trot. The home and 432 acres were purchased at an auction by Sidney Pryor Smith in 1846 from the Leaton heirs, and it was enlarged to give the house the familiar appearance it enjoys today. The house was used as an inn, and there was also a blacksmith shop on Brown's Creek behind the home. There were feeding racks and watering troughs for the animals. The place was also used as a mustering ground for newly enlisted Confederate soldiers. Grassland was sold in 1874 to W. D. Fullton, where Mrs. Fullton operated a post office in a back room of the home until 1888. Mail was delivered to Beechville, Grassland, and Forest Home post offices where recipients came to pick up their own letters. In 1836, it became the first voting place in the Seventh District.

Grassland was also known for the gum spring, a good spring on Brown's Creek, which, when other springs were low, would always give plenty of good water. It was called the Gum Spring for the gum barrel in the spot where the water rose to make a deeper basin.

Another historic home, situated on Moran Road just before the bridge over the Harpeth River, was built by John Motheral, a Revolutionary War

91

soldier who came to Williamson County in the early 1800s. The home, a log structure, was built with the front facing the river. Later the roadbed was changed and a double front porch added on the north side of the house. Today it faces Moran Road, and the river runs past the rear of the home. The house later passed through several hands, including that of Edward Hicks Moran, who served as magistrate from the Grassland district for thirty-three years. The home is now called Harpeth Side and is owned by J. Allen Reynolds III.

The Ring family has also played an important role in the history of Grassland and the government of Williamson County. The current county executive, Robert Ring and his family, lived with his aunt, Miss Emma Mai Ring, at Locust Guard on Moran Road. The Ring children are the seventh generation to live in the home built in 1823 as the home of Joseph and Anness Motheral. It was named for the magnificent locust trees that still grow in the yard. In the early 1900s, additions were made to the home which included Delco or battery operated lights, running water from a raised tank, and a windmill. The Ring family descends from Hiram Eleazer Ring of Ohio, who married Emaline Tennessee Motheral, one of Joseph and Anness' children, in 1849. After the death of her husband at Dover in 1858, Emaline returned to Locust Guard with her two sons. One son, Henry Hiram, served as magistrate in the Williamson County court for many years.

Several churches started in the Grassland community in the mid-nineteenth century and continue active today. Some of those churches are the Bethlehem United Methodist Church, Grassland Baptist, and the Berry Chapel Church of Christ. The Bethlehem United Methodist Church was organized in 1848 by members of both the Pleasant Hill Methodist Church on Sneed Road in the Ash Grove community and the old Beech Grove Methodist Church also on Sneed Road. Land on McCutcheon's Creek was given for the church in 1848 and the original building faced west, with the two doors in front—one for the men, one for the women. In 1911, the church was moved to its present site. The present church building and Sunday school classrooms were completed and dedicated March 31, 1963, and has been in continuous use since 1848, with the exception of some years during the Civil War.

Berry (not Berrys) Chapel Church of Christ began in the 1880s when members met in a one-room school on the corner of Hillsboro Road and Spencer Creek Road. In 1895, Berry Hamilton donated land on the corner of Berry Chapel and Hillsboro Road, and the church, consisting of one room, was built. There was not a baptistry so new members were baptized in the Harpeth River. In 1953 the church was renovated and an educational building constructed in 1963. A fire destroyed the main building in 1964, but the church was rebuilt and dedicated in September 1965.

Grassland Baptist, one of the newest churches, was constituted in January 1972. It began as a mission church of Nashville's Radnor Baptist Church in 1968. Before that, the Baptists held Vacation Bible School in a tent in the Meadowgreen subdivision in 1965, with prayer meetings held at the homes of members of Walker Memorial Baptist Church who lived in the Grassland area. In 1968, Radnor Baptist began the sponsorship of the mission church with worship services conducted first in a private home and later in the gym at Grassland School. A small chapel was constructed in 1970 and the congregation changed from mission status in 1972, with the present church being dedicated in May 1974. The Reverend Verlon Moore was the first full-time minister.

Schools played an important role in the growth of Grassland. One of the first was Sunnyside School, located where the Greater Pleasant View Baptist Church now stands on Hillsboro Road. This gave way in 1911 to the Grassland School, situated high on a hill about a mile south of the Sunnyside School. While Sunnyside was an ungraded school, Grassland ran through the eighth grade. In 1921, Miss Emma Mai Ring began her long and illustrious career with the Grassland School as both teacher and principal. It was a known fact that Miss Emma Mai's students were exceptionally well prepared for classes at Franklin High School. The present Grassland Elementary School was begun in 1950. To this date, it has a very active community club and Balloon Day is an annual event each fall to teach children about weather currents by sending hundreds of balloons aloft to see which balloon travels the farthest. At one time there was a school for black children. It was made of rocks, nestled in the hills off Hillsboro Road, and called "Old Rocky."

The sawmill was run by M. C. Yeargin and situated where Harpeth Valley Farm is now located on Hillsboro Road. It was later moved behind what is now the C. Y. Market, near a home owned by the Stanley family. According to M. C. Yeargin's son, Harold, Jeff Moran and Ben Hughes were the two largest landholders in the community when he was growing up. The Moran boys had a pony that liked to jump the tollgate on Hillsboro Road. One time, the pony was jumping the gate while it was being raised and flipped both pony and rider over backwards. Fortunately, neither were seriously injured. A gristmill was near the Moran house, near the Harpeth

River Rest.

River, and Moran had scales for weighing hogs and cattle before they went to market in Nashville.

Tom Henry Leigh lived in a two-story home where C. Y. Market is now located, and he had fields of strawberries and blackberries which young-sters in Grassland enjoyed picking. In later years, when his sight was failing, he would come to Franklin by pony cart. The pony was a well-trained animal and if he met anyone coming the other direction, the pony would pull the cart off to the side of the road, resuming his journey after the other vehicle had passed.

The Grassland area had one of Franklin's early subdivisions in the 1960s when Meadowgreen was built on Hillsboro Road. The old and the new meet just behind a new industry in Grassland, the Pepper Patch, which turns out jams, jellies and Tipsy Cakes for worldwide distribution. Just over the hill from his home stands the comfortable new homes in River Rest. Behind one of these homes, overlooking the Grassland area, are two small gravestones, one for John Stuart, 1725-1799, father of Judge Thomas Stuart, judge of the Fourth Circuit District, which included Williamson County, in 1809; the second is for Charles Nash, age forty-seven. The date is possibly 1826. Youngsters in River Rest often play amidst these historical markers.

26

Greenbrier

GRAND OLE OPRY PIONEER JUDGE HAY
RELATED TO EARLY GREENBRIER SETTLERS

THE GREENBRIER COMMUNITY, like so many others in Williamson County, has a name of undetermined origin. Greenbrier is located in the southwest portion of the county, close to the Maury County line. The name may have come from the Greenbrier River in Virginia, which is identified on a map of 1796. There is also a Greenbrier in Robertson County.

Elijah Fox and his wife Priscilla journeyed to the Lick Creek area, via Holly Tree Gap, coming from North Carolina in 1827. Another member of the family, Hugh Fox, came with his family by oxcart. He was nine years old at the time, and he carried the family skillet with him. He is the great grandfather of attorney Tom Fox. "Cilla Spring" on the Greenbrier Road is named for Priscilla Fox.

The first Hay child to be born in the county was Pleasant Hay, born to William and Frances Hay in 1817 in the Greenbrier community. This was the first of eight children, and William Hay went on to become a constable in the Second Civil District. The name turned up in later years on the music scene, with the Solemn Old Judge, Judge Hay from the Grand Ole Opry, who was related to the Hay family in Greenbrier.

The name Younger was among the early settlers, but their descendants moved to Missouri in the 1800s and became infamous as part of the Younger gang. In 1784, three Thompson brothers headed west from North Carolina. One came to White Oak (the Greenbrier area) for hunting and fishing, the other to Spring Hill for farming, and a third went further south to Alabama. Other settlers include the Wakefield, Parham, Prowell, Skelly,

Morton, Satterfield, and Warf families. Checking census records of 1860, it is interesting to note the occupations of Greenbrier residents: stonemason, farmer, wagon maker, carpenter, saddler, blacksmith, and shoemaker.

The early settlers who came from North Carolina came first to the Nashville area but decided against settling on the Cumberland River. They were afraid of the disease often caused from living near a lowland area, so they headed further west toward Greenbrier and settled on the familiar ridgeland to which they were accustomed. As a result, they had to work harder to eke out a living, but there was plenty of timber to be had for building, and possibly, a cash crop.

At the foot of Greenbrier Road and Lick Creek Road is the community of White Oak, part of the Greenbrier area. In 1876, the White Oak post office was created by the United States government, with George W. Thompson as the first postmaster. The post office at that time was located in the Thompson home. Later, his daughter Mrs. O. B. Sears was the postmistress when the post office was in the barn behind the house. Four generations of Thompsons have run the general store, and the late Doug Thompson was the fourth generation to farm the 331 acres across from the store. A lot of the land is in timber, and Doug's wife Ethel is still managing the farm. Besides the staple items every store carries, Thompson's Store sold all types of shoes and wire. They sold wire by the trailer load to seven different counties. And some of the oldtime shoes sold were most unusual. They were copper toed, and they were made in one style, not one for the right or left foot. In fact, the men would switch shoes each day to keep them from wearing out in the same place. They were also put together with wooden pegs.

In April 1909, a tornado completely demolished part of the house and blew away the store. After the storm, people would find one of these unique shoes, then hunt for a mate to it. Things were strewn all around: a plug of tobacco from the store was found in the Garrison community, and a two-horse wagon was blown across Lick Creek Road and wound up on the other side in an upright position. At the house, Doug Thompson's brother "Boss" Thompson was asleep when the storm went through but managed to get out of the room just before the roof came crashing through into his bedroom. The house and store were rebuilt and it was back to business as usual.

Supplies for the store were purchased in Nashville, trading local products for staples. By horse and wagon, it was a two-day trip, with an overnight stop at Forest Home. The Middle Tennessee Railroad brought some supplies until its demise in the 1920s. The Thompsons bought a truck in the 1930s to make the trip easier. During World War II, scarce items such as cigarettes and lard were sold right off the truck after a return trip from Nashville. Lard was especially in demand, with people scooping it right out of the barrels off the truck. This store, which had been so much a part of this community, closed after the death of Doug Thompson in 1982. It is still standing and used as a private home.

Greenbrier was one of the few places in Williamson County to have an early twelve-grade school. This was a one-room school, which gave way to a two-room structure which held eight grades. The second school was built close to the first one, and it is now used as a community clubhouse. Greenbrier boys did something for pleasure besides working on farms or in the log woods. They loved to play baseball and basketball. They were even part of the Williamson County All Star team in the 1930s.

Doug Thompson was on the White Oak team, and when he was sixteen years old, the team was playing at Little Rock Mills in Hickman County. He pitched a no hitter in the morning game and then came back that afternoon and pitched another full game. The strain was too much for his young growing arm, and he never pitched another game, playing second base instead. They also had a basketball team of note, with Milton Fox as one of the star players.

The Greenbrier Methodist Church, on top of the hill on Greenbrier Road, was first started in 1894 and built on land given by Thomas Prowell. Later, more land was given by John B. Fox for use as a cemetery which surrounds the church. The tornado which blew down Thompson's Store in 1909 also wrecked the church which was rebuilt, then remodeled again in 1921. The church has seen many singing quartets started there, including one headed by Willie Fox. They used to have Children's Day and Dedication Sunday the first Sunday in June, and the tradition of Dedication Day is still carried on.

The community gristmill was just behind the Thompson house, and Doug Thompson started out at the age of twelve, building the fire for the steam engine to run the mill, and it was his responsibility to keep it running all day. The blacksmith shop was near the store. Tom Gordon was the casket maker, making his products at the store. His son Ab Gordon made the sorghum.

For years, residents have found good fishing for bass, bluegill, sunperch, and catfish in the waters of Lick Creek. There was better farming by

Greenbrier Methodist Church and Cemetery.

the creek than on the ridge. In the 1950s and 1960s, people began to leave the area, as evidenced by a decline in the membership of the Greenbrier church, but with the coming of the 1990s, folks seem to head back to the quieter life which can be found in communities like Greenbrier.

27

Harpeth

THE HARPETH COMMUNITY, located south of Franklin on Lewisburg Pike, has in its background Williamson County's most notorious outlaw of the mid-1880s as well as the histories of two churches, which started in the early 1800s and are still active today. One of the earliest settlers was John Cowles, who was born in Virginia in 1801, came to Tennessee in 1825, and located near the present location of Cowles Chapel. He was a farmer, school teacher, and member of the Methodist Episcopal Church.

Sometime between 1825 and 1830, Oscar Reams gave three acres of land on what is now Critz Lane (then called Lower Thompson Road), about a fourth of a mile off Lewisburg Pike, to be used for a church. The church was called Prospect Methodist Church, but it was also used as a schoolhouse during the week. Parishioners and students alike sat on long wooden benches and the room was heated with an open fireplace. Church records, now in the possession of Tom Stoddard, indicate the first member of the Prospect Church joined in 1827 and the last in 1868. At one time, the congregation had as little as eighty-two cents in its treasury.

In August 1871, Cowles bought the estate of a Mr. Reams and deeded one and one-half acres of land in exchange for three acres previously given. This one and one-half acres was for the new church, renamed Cowles Chapel. Some of the church pews built in 1871 are still in use today. Cowles became the first member of the new Cowles Chapel Church in 1871. When the church was constructed, there were two doors in the entrance, one for use by the men and one for the women, and a rail down the middle to separate the sexes. The ministers, often college students from Vanderbilt, were then, and are still, considered circuit-riding preachers on the Burwood-Thompson Station Cowles Chapel circuit. W. P. Scales, a member of the church and teacher at the Harpeth School, gave the land for a school yard. The nearby West Harpeth Creek has a tendency to rise and would often flood Cowles Chapel Church so members would be forced to meet at the school. In the early 1950s, members made a decision to jack up the building and the big question was, "How high?" They decided to make it higher than most of the congregation deemed necessary and it was a good thing they did, for the next heavy rain which came brought water which rose to the highest level without ever getting into the church proper. The large cross outside the church was used as a setting for an Easter sunrise service in the 1970s and still stands.

The other church in Harpeth, the New Hope Presbyterian just up the road on Lewisburg Pike, was first called the Old Ridge Meeting House because it was built on the Ridge, a geographical formation which separates the drainage between the Harpeth and Duck Rivers. First services were conducted as brush arbor meetings under the trees. Then a small wooden building was used in 1806 when the Reverend Duncan Brown from South Carolina came and organized New Hope Church about a mile north of Old Ridge. This structure was initially also called Ridge Meeting House but was later changed to New Hope. It is said that several of the Scotch and Scotch-Irish members, namely the Andersons, were homesick for their church "New Hope" back in Hillsboro, North Carolina. The present structure was completed in 1869 on land donated by James S. Williams. Hand tools were used to form the huge slabs for the flooring, and the head of each family made the bench for his family to use and nailed the bench to the floor. People would come from as far away as Spring Hill to the New Hope Church. Both the Cowles Chapel and New Hope Churches held revival meetings during the summer months.

Harpeth School served the educational needs of the youngsters. The first building, across from Critz Lane, later burned and the building on Lewisburg Pike was started around 1916. W. P. Scales was one of the teachers, as well as the basketball and baseball coach. Scales had a reputation for being an excellent disciplinarian. Children often had to cut their own switches for paddling purposes, and it's told that if parents disagreed with his discipline, he gave the parents a whack or two. The school has seen several changes over the

New Hope Presbyterian Church.

years and is now the Harpeth Valley Baptist Church.

The blacksmith shop was run by Polk Jordan, and the gristmill by Sam Deason. The store at Harpeth was first owned by Tom Wallace and later by Sam Fleming. When he was a boy, Fleming would operate the cotton gin behind the store. Wallace lost a hand in an accident at the cotton gin, moving to Franklin to serve as county court clerk when Fleming took over the day-to-day operations.

The Harpeth community is set between several large hills on Lewisburg Pike. One known as Murrell Hill is home of the notorious outlaw John A. Murrell. Born in Williamson County in 1804, Murrell was tried in a Franklin court in April 1823, found guilty of riot, and fined. He then went on to become one of the most notorious outlaws in the country, specializing in slave stealing. One legend has it that he hid out in a cave near Sumner's Knob in the Triune area and planned a rebellion of local slaves while he was in hiding. He was to start at the nearby Jim Jones' plantation in Triune and have the rebellion spread to the surrounding area. His real plan was to get the slaves to follow him across the state line and hold them at his property. A man on the Jones' plantation knew what was happening, told Jones, and Murrell was captured and locked in a small room of the Palmore house located in Rutherford County. Murrell escaped, hid out, but was captured by John S. Russwurm of Triune.

During the Civil War, on another hill, people would gather to watch the soldiers come down Columbia Pike. One farm, once belonging to Walter Anderson, was the last portion of a large Revolutionary War land grant belonging to his forefathers. Lewisburg Pike was at one time a toll road, with one toll gate directly across from Anderson's home. Young men, after the age of twenty-one, were responsible for the section of road fronting their homeplace. They were to keep the road in good shape, find someone to do it for them, or were forced to pay a fine to the county.

The Harpeth community, while never large, still has church members who have attended New Hope Presbyterian Church and Cowles Chapel for generations, continuing the tradition and carrying on the family names in the Harpeth community.

28

Kingfield

SITE OF
SEVENTH-DAY ADVENTIST CHURCH

T HE COMMUNITY OF KINGFIELD is located near Leiper's Fork in the western part of the county. It's a small community on a ridge over-looking a creek. Like so many areas, it was settled in the early 1800s, and named for Ransom King. When Ransom King died in 1865, he left a tract of land of 150 acres in the first district, Kingfield area. Settlers came to Kingfield because they wanted to raise a little patch of corn and to live as they chose. It is one of only two areas in the county with a Seventh-Day Adventist Church, the other being the corner of Coleman Road and Columbia Avenue.

The Adventists came as missionaries in the early 1900s starting both the church and the nearby school. One man in particular, during a World War I bond drive, noted that many of the Kingfield folks were unable to read and write, so he stayed in the community and started the Kingfield Industrial School, which was in existence from 1918 until 1923. Other children went to Pond School, which went through the eighth grade, and those wanting to further their education went to high school either in Leiper's Fork or Franklin. In addition to the Seventh-Day Adventist Church, there is also a Pond Church of Christ. A Jesus Only Church was in Kingfield during the 1950s. The Adventist Church started with five charter members, and their membership today numbers only about thirty, with some family members staying and others leaving the community.

The prime industry in a community surrounded by trees was the sawmill industry, with up to four mills in Kingfield. Tom Cash ran a

104

sawmill on some land he purchased in the 1930s and, after the timber ran out, he sold the property. Sam and Noble King ran another mill, near King's Grocery, the community gathering place. Billy Goodman and his father came from White Bluff to run a mill, but they were only in business for a year. Another mill, run by Thomas Ham, was located near Fernvale. At one time, there was a shingle mill and a gristmill operating in the area, but there were no blacksmith shops. The two blacksmith shops nearby were located in Leiper's Fork.

The most prominent store in Kingfield was one run by Noble and Vera King. Actually, she ran the store for him. They sold dry goods, plow points, shoes, ready to wear, and toys, in addition to the usual grocery items. From 1943 to 1977, Vera would make trips to Nashville each Monday, visiting four or five wholesale houses to purchase supplies. Customers came over from Hickman County to shop at King's Store. The store itself was built in the 1930s and first owned by Felix King who sold the business to Alex Hargrove, who in turn sold it to the Noble Kings in 1943. Noble and Vera King had a store before that one, a smokehouse grocery, started during the depression years in the corner of their yard. Each of the residents in

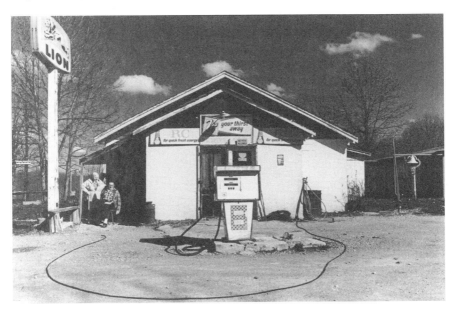

Old Holiness Church now Pewitt Store.

Kingfield had a house and garden plot, but before they could do any gardening, they had to cut a lot of trees to make room for the corn, tomatoes, green beans, and peppers which were then sold at market.

If people needed medical attention, they called either Dr. Dan German or Dr. Tandy Rice from Franklin, or one of three doctors from Hillsboro, Dr. Coles, Dr. Black, or Dr. Drake.

The late Clair Regen, a Williamson County businessman early in his career, sold kerosene refrigerators to folks in Kingfield. Vera King took one, reluctantly, when she was told to try it for a few weeks. She was sold, and she and Noble purchased this piece of modern equipment. Electricity came to Kingfield after World War II and telephones came in during the 1950s, but in order to have a phone one had to have at least six memberships with the phone company. The first automobile was an unusual one; it was called a Metz, and it was made in Hamburg, Germany, about 1918. Noble King purchased it in Franklin as a secondhand car.

The Kingfield community has families who have lived there for generations with few changes. It's a quiet place and people living there today are like their ancestors—they stay there for a chance to live as they choose.

29

Kirkland

T HE KIRKLAND COMMUNITY, located on Horton Highway between College Grove and Triune, is the homeplace of the first governor of Tennessee to come from Williamson County, Newton Cannon. The name, "Kirkland" was probably derived from the Scotch word for church by early settlers in the area. Newton Cannon, the most famous resident of the community, was born in North Carolina in 1781, coming to Middle Tennessee with his family in 1790, and settling in Kirkland. Cannon learned a saddler's trade in Franklin, later mastering the art of surveying. Before he reached the age of thirty, he knew politics would be his life's work, and in 1811 he was elected to the state senate.

Early in his political career, Cannon ran afoul of Andrew Jackson and the stern General Jackson was not one to forgive and forget. During the Indian Wars of 1813, Newton Cannon was a commander of the Tennessee Volunteers fighting the Creek Indians. Because the War Office would not support their field commanders at all times, Cannon was once forced to pay his own soldiers three month's salary out of his own pocket. This precipitated a series of angry letters to Jackson, and from the general back to Cannon. Later their paths crossed in the courtroom and on the racetrack but neither forgave the other for incidents in the Indian Wars.

In 1819, Cannon was appointed by President James Monroe to serve as one of two commissioners to negotiate a treaty with the Chickasaw Indians. Cannon's lack of formal education in his youth prompted him to become a pioneer in education for young people, especially young women. In 1828 he

107

gave land for the Harpeth Union Female Academy, a brick schoolhouse which stood for many years along the pike between Triune and Kirkland. His interest in education continued after he was elected governor, when the state legislature adopted a bill for "common schools," the predecessor to today's public schools.

In 1834, Newton Cannon was selected to be part of a constitutional convention to help revise the state's constitution and, in 1835, was elected to his first term as governor. He was reelected in 1837, running on the Whig party ticket. He tried a third time, in 1839, but his life-long nemesis, Andrew Jackson, saw to it that a Jackson protégé James K. Polk was elected governor. Two years later, in 1841, Cannon became ill while on a business trip to West Tennessee and died September 16 of that year. He is buried on his home place in Kirkland where his monument records highlights of his illustrious career from Indian fighter to governor. Newton Cannon's home passed into other families and was given by the Joe Bellenfant family to the Heritage Foundation. It was restored by Mr. and Mrs. Ron Faye, only to have vandals destroy it by fire in 1987.

Another home in Kirkland, belonging to Dr. William Smith Webb, was built in 1811 on land given to Webb by the government for services rendered as a surveyor. In 1826 he added 200 acres to his property, purchased from the state at the price of a penny an acre. Later, he purchased 160 acres for a total price of fifteen dollars. The Webb place is also the burial site of James Turner, a Revolutionary War soldier who served five tours of duty with the North Carolina army before coming to Williamson County with his family in 1808. One of his children, Mildred Turner, married Dr. William Smith Webb. James Turner died in 1835 at the age of seventy-eight and is buried on the Webb property.

James Webb, son of Mildred and William, built another beautiful home in the community, just across from the home of his parents. The house sits on a high hill and was called "Sylvan Retreat" because the hill was covered with trees. During the Civil War, Federal troops camped in front of the hill because of the cooling shade and a good spring nearby. The home has been renamed "Kirkview," is in beautifully restored condition, and is owned by James and Melody Sipes.

In addition to distinctive homes, there were several stores in Kirkland. Isham Jordan once operated a country store on the corner of 31 and 41A, where he sold everything from two-horse wagons to shoes, groceries, and bolts of material for the ladies. Jordan operated the store for forty years.

Later, Tom Seat built another store in the community. A Mr. Long ran two mills just north of the 31-41A corner. One was a steam-powered sawmill, and the other a gristmill which could boast of two millstones, one turning the other, which was said to give the meal a better flavor than that ground on steel rollers.

Blacks played an important role in Kirkland. Ellis Scales operated a general store with an undertaker's shop in the back, and he used a

McCord house at Kirkland.

two-horse wagon as his hearse. Ab Scales was remembered by both blacks and whites as a good financier and it was known by all that if one wanted to do well, he or she should call Ab Scales. White children went to schools in Triune and College Grove, while black children had their own churches and schools in Kirkland.

The Kirkland community is primarily an area of magnificent homes and truck and dairy farms, but it is best known for its most prominent citizen, Newton Cannon.

30

Leiper's Fork

EARLY HOME OF MISSOURI SENATOR
THOMAS HART BENTON

T HE COMMUNITY OF LEIPER'S FORK (OR HILLSBORO), whichever one chooses to call it, is located nine miles west of Franklin on Old Hillsboro Road. The community has existed under three names, Bentontown, Leiper's Fork, and Hillsboro. The community originated as early as 1785 when forty acres of land was granted to Hugh Leiper in what was to become Williamson County. The land was described as being on a large fork, known as Leiper's Fork, in the Harpeth River. This would seem to indicate that Hugh Leiper's parents, Andrew and Jennie, first owned this land. Hugh's brother, James, was the groom in the first wedding to take place at Fort Nashborough when he married Susan Drake in 1780. However, he never lived in Williamson County since he died as a result of wounds received in the Battle of the Bluffs in April 1781 at Fort Nashborough. Three Leiper brothers, James, Hugh, and George, were all in Middle Tennessee in 1780 and signed the Cumberland Compact.

Leiper's Fork was actually first christened "Bentontown" for the family of Thomas Hart Benton, who later served for thirty years as a U.S. senator from Missouri. Benton came to Williamson County in 1801 along with his widowed mother, brothers, and sisters on a 600-mile journey from North Carolina to claim a 3000-acre land grant given to his father who had died of "consumption," or tuberculosis, before the family left the Carolinas. The family built a sturdy home of stone and wood, a portion of which was underground to protect them from the Indians.

111

Benton was a practicing lawyer in Franklin and Nashville by 1806. In fact, court records indicate from 1809 to 1812 he was the busiest lawyer in Williamson County, and he probably would have left his mark on Tennessee history as a local lawyer except for an incident in 1813 which involved his brother Jesse and Andrew Jackson. At one time, Jackson had been a second for William Carroll in a duel against Jesse Benton, which Thomas resented. One day, in a Nashville hotel, tempers flared and evolved into a brawl with Jesse shooting Jackson and severely wounding him. He recovered, but the wound troubled him the rest of his life. Thomas and Andrew Jackson reconciled their differences, but Jesse was unable to "forgive and forget" which caused tension between the brothers. In 1815, before any forgiveness transpired, the Bentons felt it would be unwise to stay in Tennessee and left for Missouri. Thomas Hart Benton had served in the Tennessee Legislature and as a U.S. senator from Missouri and was known as "Old Bullion" for his continuing stand on sound currency.

The Bentons were not the only residents of Leiper's Fork area to run afoul of the law. In 1826, Daniel Crenshaw was convicted at the Williamson County Courthouse for stealing a horse. Included in his punishment was the branding of the initials "H. T." on his hand. Whereupon he bit the still-hot letters out of his hand and spit them on the ground.

Earlier, one of the Leiper brothers had shot and killed the infamous Big Harpe in Muhlenberg County, Kentucky. Big Harpe's head was placed on a pole to remind others in the area that "crime does not pay." Big Harpe and his brother Little Harpe terrorized inhabitants of Tennessee and Kentucky in the early 1800s. Little Harpe was eventually caught and hanged near Natchez, Mississippi.

The name of the area changed from Bentontown, after the departure of the Benton family, to Leiper's Fork, and Hillsboro, for the coming of settlers from Hillsboro, North Carolina. Other settlers include the Bennett, Hunter, Sweeney, Cunningham, Southall, Rogers, and Holland families.

The first organized church was started in 1821, on a plot of ground donated by Hugh Dobbins, and called Union Church, since all denominations were allowed to worship there. The church was located then, as now, on Old Hillsboro Road. In 1829, two preachers at the church, Joel Anderson and Andrew Craig, both Primitive Baptists, were "withdrawn" from the congregations for preaching what was considered heresy, the doctrines of Alexander Campbell. In 1830, these two men formed the first Church of

On the sign:

3 D   6

THOMAS HART BENTON

On the foundations of this house
was home of Thomas Hart Benton,
whose family came from North
Carolina in 1788. In 1809 he was
state senator. Moving to Missouri
in 1815, he became U.S. Senator in
1821, and remained in the senate
30 years. Dying at the age of 76,
in 1858, he left a record of
outstanding statesmanship.

Site of Thomas Hart Benton house foundation. (The chimneys are all that remain of a house built over the original foundation.)

Christ in the county and, in 1831, Seth Sparkman and his wife were baptized into the church, becoming the first people south of Nashville to do so. From 1821 until 1845 the original building was used for worship services, then torn down and another built on an adjoining lot. The new church was used by the Baptist, Methodist, Cumberland Presbyterian, and "Christian" denominations, each using the building once a month for their services. In 1877, the "Christians" bought out the other denominations and by 1880, the church membership numbered 200.

The Hillsboro United Methodist Church was constructed on land purchased from the Meacham family. John Meacham, Will Fulton, and a Mr. P. Hassell are responsible for the start of the church, which was a part of the Bethlehem circuit at its inception in 1910. An annex was added in 1962 to serve as a kitchen and fellowship hall.

The Hillsboro Baptist Church began as a prayer meeting January 1961 at the home of Mr. and Mrs. J. W. Shelby on Waddell Hollow Road. In the spring of that same year, the Nashville Baptist Association purchased a lot on Old Hillsboro Road, where the present structure stands, and conducted a tent meeting on the site. A garage was converted into a meeting place in September 1961, under the sponsorship of Glendale Baptist Church. A building was finally started the next year and dedicated in June with J. C. Spencer as the first pastor.

The residents of Hillsboro were very interested in the education of their young people. The Hillsboro School was started as a private academy in 1891 by William Anderson. The school was a three-room structure on Old Highway 96. Next to the school was the home of the Anderson family which was also used as a dormitory for female students while the boys stayed at a home across the street. Boarding facilities were a necessity as there were students from Nashville, Franklin, Columbia, Carter's Creek, Theta, and Brentwood, among others, though most came from Leiper's Fork. Yearly tuition was $10 for primary grades, $22.50 for high school, and board was $9 and $10 a year. Classes were taught in music, elocution, Latin, Greek, and geography. Church attendance was required and parents were asked not to interfere with the school's discipline. In 1901, Anderson was called to become president of Nashville Bible School, later David Lipscomb College.

The Hillsboro School started as a private institution until 1905 when the county took it over. In 1930, lightning struck the building and it burned to the ground. A new school was built by the citizens of the community and later bought by the county. A "bus" of sorts ran from the western part of the county to the school. Actually, it was a flatbed truck, driven by the principal Orgain Seay. The school building and enrollment continued to grow with the new classrooms, and a cafeteria and science facilities were added over the years. In 1982, grades K through 8 moved into a new building on Pinewood Road, while the other grades were transferred to other county high schools.

April 29, 1909, was a day of fearful terror for residents of the community. At eleven o'clock that night, after an unusually hot day, a killer tornado ripped through the area. One home, which it destroyed, was that of Mr. and Mrs. Joe Jones, who lived there with their fourteen children and grandchildren. The Jones' family members were literally blown out of their house by the wind. When Mr. Jones went back into the house to retrieve his two-year-old daughter Margaret, the wind blew her into his arms. When the harsh winds finally calmed, he began calling his children, not knowing how many were still alive. One by one they came to answer their names. They were covered with blood and mud, but all were alive. Not so fortunate were the Jeff Marlins. Their home was totally destroyed and three sons were killed. Mr. Marlin was seriously injured and Mrs. Marlin later died of her injuries. In Sweeney Hollow, Mrs. Matt Sweeney and Golden Coleman were both killed. At nearby Beechwood Hall, residents lost twenty trees from the grounds and recall the tornado seemed to leap over the house before touching down at Hillsboro.

Alex Black operated a store in Leiper's Fork for thirty-eight years, starting in 1869. It also housed the post office, established in the rear of the store. His wife was postmistress for thirty-two years. Early records indicate George A. Conn was postmaster at Leiper's Fork from 1845 until 1849, and William A. Rodgers postmaster in 1851.

The Leiper's Fork Bank was located the corner of Old Hillsboro Road and the road to Fernvale. The bank opened in 1912 and closed its doors for the final time in 1932, but none of its customers lost a penny from its demise. The bank burned about four years ago.

One business has been on the outskirts of the community for years and yet is very much a part of all the activities. Green's Store, on Old Hillsboro Road, was started over fifty years ago by Herman Green. The store has always sold general merchandise, hardware items, and in the early days, horse and cattle feed. Folks would come into the store to swap tales around the potbellied stove and check out the collection of rattlesnake skins Green had hanging on his wall. Before Herman Green had the store, it was owned by a Mr. Pigue and today it serves as a restaurant and songwriters' haven.

A water system came through Hillsboro to Franklin, pumping water from the springs beyond Hillsboro. The reservoir is located on Carter's Creek Pike, and the pumping station is housed in several small brick buildings along Carter's Creek Pike.

In the mid-nineteenth century, medical care came from a local resident, Dr. George Bennett Hunter, who was named for his maternal uncle, George Bennett, a Hillsboro pioneer settler. Hunter studied medicine in Philadelphia, and returned to his home community. He was unable to serve in the Confederate army because of an injury which occurred as a result of a fall from a horse, but he still worked very hard, being in the saddle day and night, treating the patients of Williamson County.

The main entrance to the community, Old Hillsboro Road, was for many years a toll road, with the tollgate located at the bottom of the hill coming into town. The tollhouse was owned by the South Harpeth Turnpike Company and was in use until 1927 when county roads became free public roads. The building was torn down in the late 1970s and some of the lumber used in a private home.

Whether it's called Leiper's Fork, Hillsboro, or Bentontown, this community is proud of its heritage and continues to be a gracious place to live away from the faster pace of the city, yet close to all the activities.

31

Liberty

LIBERTY CHURCH FOUNDED BY
EARLY SETTLER GREEN HILL

THE LIBERTY COMMUNITY, which grew up around the Liberty Methodist Church, was once a vital part of the northern part of the county. In the early days, Liberty was oriented towards Nolensville, where the post office and trading post were located. Later Brentwood took over that position. The only business in the community was Hamer's Store, which stood at the corner of Concord and Liberty Church Roads and closed in the early 1900s. However, when there was a post office at Liberty in the late 1800s, it was called Benbrook and situated inside Hamer's Store.

The small Liberty Church had a proud moment early in its history. In 1808, it was the host church for the Western Conference of the Methodist Church, with both Bishops McKendree and Asbury in attendance. There were seven districts and eighty preachers present.

The first reference to the Liberty Meeting House was in the July 1804 minutes of the Williamson County Court, and the first site possibly being on property now owned by T. Vance Little. There is a good chance that until 1806 the congregation met in a community meeting house. In 1837 an acre of land was donated by John Hamer to the trustees of the church, and tradition has it the first church building was a log structure. When the present church was built, the logs were moved to the Hamer place and are now used as a barn. The Liberty Church, founded by Green Hill, is the mother church of all the other Methodist churches in the area. In the late 1800s it was on a circuit with the Nolensville, Hebron, and Kedron churches. Today, the Liberty Church is under the jurisdiction of the History and Archives

117

Liberty Community Club.

Commission of the Tennessee Conference and services are occasionally held in the building.

A number of early settlers made up the Liberty community—among them the Hill, Hunt, Hamer, Bell, Edmondson, Brown, Winstead, Fly, and Primm families. The community took its name from the North Carolina home of one of these early settlers, Green Hill, whose home had been named Liberty Hill before he settled in Williamson County in 1799. His family was one of wealth and influence in North Carolina, and as a lay preacher, he was instrumental in spreading Methodism in North Carolina and Tennessee. This was probably his main reason for coming to Tennessee. A Revolutionary War colonel, he came to Fort Nashborough in 1796, living there until his home, Liberty Hill, was completed. His home stood until the 1920s when it was torn down.

William Winstead was the first of his family to appear in the Williamson County record books, and he died in 1831. In the 1850s, John Matthew Winstead, nephew of William, built Pleasant Hill, a magnificent antebellum home, which is still standing today. It was built to face south, towards the old Nolensville-Franklin Pike. On the Pleasant Hill property is a log home, in fact several, where early Winstead settlers lived before the grand mansion was built.

One of the early trustees of the Liberty Church was John Fly. He later moved to Maury County and settled what is known as Fly Station. However, when he died, he was buried in Williamson County on Ragsdale Road. Several Hamer families are on early Williamson County tax records, the earliest being Daniel, who paid taxes in 1802. Others were John Hamer and Rebecca Hamer.

Possibly the first family in the community was the Edmondson family, John Edmondson coming from Virginia. The land had been deeded to him by his uncle. This man, also named John Edmondson, had the distinction of being the only man in the American Revolution shot by a ramrod. At the Battle of Kings Mountain, a British soldier, in his haste, failed to remove the ramrod from his muzzle loader before firing it into the ranks. Edmondson received the shot but lived to tell about it. Edmondson land is still in the family.

Jonathan Hunt, father of early settler Gersham Hunt, commanded a company during the Revolutionary War and is said to have been the first man to receive General George Washington upon his arrival at Salisbury, North Carolina. When Jonathan's son Gersham came to Liberty in the late 1700s, he was leader of the militia company from his district and also a justice of the peace.

For its small size, Liberty has been the site of at least four schools. One of the earliest was Ellis School, just north of the church. Another was Beech Grove School and another Edmondson School, located on Edmondson property. The school was a log structure and used in later years as a corncrib. Liberty School was opened in 1900, on land donated by W. L. and Cynthia Fly. One of Williamson County's foremost teachers, Miss Emma Mai Ring, taught at the Liberty School, staying with Hugh Edmondson. The children were responsible for keeping the building and grounds clean. The building was never locked and the first boy at school in the morning during the winter months was responsible for making the fire in the woodstove. The school consisted of one room and one teacher until the fall of 1914, when a second room and a second teacher were added. The school remained open until 1940 and has since been used as a community center and Sunday school annex for the church. There was possibly a fifth school, Bell School, which was near the early Liberty Meeting House before the church was built, and may have had as many as twenty pupils.

In later years, the Liberty Church was known throughout the county for its summer lawn festivals. Families, friends, aspiring politicians, and everyone who was anyone would come to these summer activities. The Liberty Church continues today, and while its membership hasn't grown, many members are descendants of the founders. Some of the early families still live in Liberty, some on the same property owned by their ancestors. It's nice to feel a sense of continuity about the Liberty community.

32

Liberty Hill

COMMUNITY SITUATED NEAR TURNBULL CREEK

L IBERTY HILL is located on Old Cox Pike and Crow Cut Road past Fairview. Three elementary schools have been in the community, one built in the 1920s, another in the 1930s. Both these burned, possibly as the result of woodstove fires which overheated. These schools went from the first through the eighth grades, with students continuing their education at Hillsboro or Fairview High Schools.

Around 1915, a missionary Baptist church was located in the community, but the only church at the present time is the Church of Christ, which was built about 1950 and has been remodeled since then. In the summer of 1917, there was a religious debate in Liberty Hill between the Baptists and the Church of Christ. The debate had the atmosphere of a political rally with a concession stand selling sandwiches and soda pop, an unusual sight for 1917. Each side thought they had won, but Pink Daugherty, spokesman for the Baptist side and well-known music teacher in western Williamson County, was sure he was the victor.

Liberty Hill flourished around the turn of the century with a gristmill, sawmill, general store, stave mill and blacksmith shop. All the businesses were owned at one time or another by Will Sullivan who was, at that time, the most prominent man in the community. A second gristmill was run by W. J. Fisher and later purchased by Earl Lampley. The mill was moved to another part of Turnbull Creek in the 1920s and torn down in 1984. The blacksmith shop, run by George Overbey, was located at Will Sullivan's store. The stave mill turned out barrel staves for flour, pickle, and whiskey barrels. Families whose names are familiar in Liberty Hill are Lampley, Sullivan, Spicer, Dunnigan, Lankford, Buttrey, Tomlinson, Overbey, Bethshears, Curtis, and Cunningham.

There is quite a bit of truck gardening done in the area. Years ago, tomatoes were delivered to Martin Tohrner's in Franklin. Luda Spicer Fisher told of the time she and family members spent a hot summer's day culling tomatoes to take to market. They managed to get ninety-nine bushel baskets of extra good tomatoes, free from any blemish or spot. When Tohrner saw them, he was delighted with the quality and told them to bring in one more basket so they would have an even 100. Sorghum molasses was also made in Liberty Hill. The day George Lampley turned eighty-one, he managed to make 200 buckets in one day, not an easy task! Currently there is some row crop farming, cattle and hog raising, and the area has always been good timber country.

Turnbull Creek runs near the Liberty Hill community, and there is a delightful story as to how Turnbull Creek got its name. Seems that in the days of oxcarts and no bridges to cross the creek, two men were driving a team of oxen across the creek. The creek proved to be deeper than the men thought. One got out of the cart and said, "Turn the bulls around." Legend or fact, it's a good story.

Liberty Hill School.

Before the days of county road crews, the man who put up the money to gravel and grade a county road had the road named for him. Cox Pike was named for P. E. Cox in the 1920s.

The Liberty Hill community has several residents who have dedicated their lives to teaching youngsters in western Williamson County. Luda Fisher retired after forty-two years of teaching. She taught four years at the Liberty Hill School. She also taught at Aden, Naomi, New Hope, Triangle, and the old Fairview High School. She would often walk from her home to the Naomi School, or bike to New Hope. Sometimes she boarded in Fairview if she knew she'd be teaching more than a few days. The late Mildred Bethshears was raised in Liberty Hill and taught some in Craigfield, but spent most of her teaching career in Iowa.

Liberty Hill has never been a large or prosperous community. It is situated so close to the Dickson County line that most of the residents do their shopping in Dickson, but it has been part of the history of Williamson County, and it is made up of hardworking folks who care about their families and their neighbors.

33

Millview

THE MILLVIEW COMMUNITY, located on Arno Road, is made up of several churches, a general store, and a very active community club, which is still going strong after forty years. Millview was named for John N. House's mill on the Harpeth River and until recently, ruins of the mill could be seen from the bridge across the river. The first bridge was a covered wooden bridge, which was later replaced by an arched iron bridge. In 1975, Arno Road was widened and a modern concrete bridge replaced the narrow, iron structure.

Two stores served the community's grocery needs. Mrs. Alma Jordan and her husband ran one store and the other was owned by Mr. and Mrs. Mathis, who sold it to Mr. and Mrs. Russell Zimmerman in 1950, and since 1956 it has seen several different owners.

Lankford School, named for the family who donated the land, educated youngsters in the area through the late 1940s. It was one of the first schools to serve hot lunches to its students. This was a project of the PTA, to make sure all the youngsters had warm, healthful meals during the school days. Black children attended school in a building on Arno Road. The same building was also used as a place of worship for members of the Millview Church of Christ.

The first Millview Church of Christ location was in the home of Mrs. Louvina Talley, where members, eight or ten in number, would meet on Sunday afternoons starting in 1953. From there they moved to the schoolhouse which had educated black children in the community. In 1971, the congregation built a new brick building at the corner of Highway 96 East and North Chapel Roads. Today, the congregation has grown from 10 to over 250 per Sunday.

A familiar landmark in Millview is the Epworth United Methodist Church, on Arno Road, just past the bridge. The present church was founded in 1909 as the result of the consolidation of two churches, Thomas Church and North Chapel. The Thomas Church dated back to 1853 and was a log house built on the site of an old meeting house. North Chapel was started in 1867 and was located in a frame house. Both Thomas Church and North Chapel were strong, active, vital forces in a growing community. Revivals or "protracted meetings" as they were called, were held, as were Children's Day activities and Quarterly Conferences, and there were close ties between both churches. In the early 1900s Thomas Church was in bad repair, while attendance was slipping at North Chapel, which led parishioners of both churches to a decision to consolidate.

The Epworth Church grew from these two. The church was built on land donated by Jess and Mittie Toon Pierce and bricks from Thomas Church were used in the construction, as was a portion of the chancel rail. Church members worshiped at North Chapel during the construction, and the North Chapel pulpit was added to the Epworth Church. The Epworth Church was dedicated in April 1909 as a Circuit church. Festivities for the day included a dinner on the ground, but as so often happens with Tennessee springtime activities, it was cold and spitting snow, so members moved across the road to Riverside and had their dinner indoors. The church grew and prospered and, in 1952, with the help of the young adult class, six classrooms, a kitchen, and nursery were added. In 1953 land was donated by Miss Mary Hatcher for a parsonage. Then, with the parsonage, Sunday school rooms, a daily Vacation Bible School in the summer, and community support, the church became a Charge church, with a full-time minister. One of the major summer events for the community, which occurred each year at the Epworth United Methodist Church, was the annual lawn festival, many of which were held on the lawn at Riverside. It was a time of auctions—jam cakes selling for as much as thirty dollars each, country hams, and some of the best food ever turned out by Williamson County's best cooks. In 1960, the Epworth Church received the honor of "Rural Church of the Year" from the Tennessee Annual Conference and, in 1977, more additions were made to the ever-growing congregation with tennis and basketball courts for the young people.

In 1951, the Millview Community Club was begun with the following long-range objectives in mind: to help make the community a better place to live, to build a recreational center for the youth, to support charity groups, to improve farms and homes, and to participate in the work of the community, county, state, and nation. Lofty ideals, but forty-three years later they are still very active, and a vital force in Millview. The community club first met at Lankford School in August 1952 and was known appropriately as the Lankford Community Club. Among the fifty-three people at the first meeting were prominent names in Millview such as T. W. Bratten, Jackson Noland, Walter Bond, Dave Alexander, Leonard Vaden, R. R. Zimmerman, W. P. Ladd, Ada Floyd, Percy Sparkman, Mrs. Frank Eslick, and Miss Mary Hatcher, to name just a few. They moved over to the

The beautiful antebellum home, Riverside, which takes its name from the Harpeth River, was lovingly built by Beverly Barksdale Toon, who came to Williamson County in 1811. The house was completed for Toon and his wife, the former Sarah Nolen in 1857, and constructed of timber from nearby forests and brick kilned on the property. During the Civil War, family silver was buried in the backyard, and those precious country hams were kept safe under the house on the rock foundation. During the war, an incident occurred when a Yankee officer came and threatened to burn down the house. When Toon asked to talk to the officer, Toon gave the Masonic sign, which saved Riverside from destruction. The house moved out of the family from 1916 until 1923 when it was returned to descendants. Today it is the home of Jimmy and Sarah Bratton Lillard and her family, descendants of the original owners.

Epworth Methodist Church, and in February 1954, the name was changed to the Millview Community Club. Ten years later, on August 1, 1964, land was purchased from Mr. and Mrs. B. E. Givens on the corner of Trinity-Peytonsville and Arno Roads, and it became Millview Community Club, incorporated, with a new clubhouse. Since then a swimming pool has been added and club members still meet once a month with activities for the whole family.

In 1984, the Epworth Church celebrated its seventy-fifth anniversary since its inception in 1909. The Millview Community Club is going strong, and it's nice to know that when so many lifestyles are changing and so many small communities may be listed on the map but no longer exist in reality, that the Millview community still has a firm sense of family ties and unity. The original goal of the community club, to make the area a better place to live, seems to have been effective.

34

Mudsink

THE COMMUNITY OF MUDSINK shares its charming, descriptive name with roads and other communities in Williamson County, such as Hen Peck Lane, Goosecreek By-Pass, Poor House Hollow Road, and Bending Chestnut. Mudsink is located at the intersection of Clovercroft and Murfreesboro Roads. It was given the name because it is such a low place in the road and the waters from nearby Watson Creek would often flood. Wagoners were told to be wary driving their loads through the area. According to legend, wagons and teams were known to disappear, never to be seen again.

One settler in the mid-1880s was B. O. Watson, and according to an article in the *Western Weekly Review*, Watson sold a 640-acre farm in 1855. At that time a house was being built on the property. The house was described as fifty-one square feet, with twenty-three foot ells. According to the notice, there were "plenty of first rate Negro houses and barns, a new gin house, first rate tobacco barn and etc. Well watered with five or six springs." The house stood until it was torn down in 1977 to make way for Breckenridge South subdivision.

A historical marker on Murfreesboro Road, just before Clovercroft Road, marks the McConnico Meeting House. This is the historic site of the first formal church in Williamson County and the third church constituted south of Nashville. Garner McConnico was born in Lunenberg County, Virginia, in 1771. As a young boy, his mother encouraged him to attend a nearby tent meeting with her. The preacher was an Englishman and a former soldier in the British army. The McConnico family had been forced

The Williams' house, over 150 years old.

so often to hide from the British during the Revolutionary War, young Garner was determined not to like or listen to the preacher. But the message from this man was so powerful, it overwhelmed his resistance, and the boy found himself at the close of the service standing next to the preacher. McConnico joined the Baptist Church in 1788, at the age of seventeen. At eighteen, he married the former Mary Walker, and in 1795, the two of them left Virginia and traveled to Davidson County, Tennessee. They moved to Williamson County two years later in 1797, where they built a beautiful home in the Virginia fashion. He left his mark on the religious community of Middle Tennessee when he founded the Big Harpeth Church on the Saturday before the fourth Sunday in May 1800. He was one of twenty members. The first church was a log building where the congregation sat on puncheon, or split-log benches. The building stood on land donated by Dan German.

Garner McConnico was a man of a dominant presence and a powerful voice. He also kept his promises. He had promised to speak to his congregation under the shade trees near the Murfreesboro Road Bridge, but the Harpeth River was at flood stage, and they could not get across the waters.

So, he preached his sermon on one side of the river, and the congregation, on the other side, didn't miss a word over the rushing waters. He was conducting one meeting during the earthquake of 1811, the effects of which were felt in Middle Tennessee. During the preaching, there was a cry that the house was sinking, and the entire congregation began to panic. Some ran away shouting "He's coming! He's coming!" Some fell out of the gallery, and some lay crying on the floor. One man in desperation tried to get through a large chink between the logs of the house, but he didn't make it and had to be pulled back.

McConnico died in 1833 at his home and is buried at the Kinnard Cemetery in Arno, along with his daughter Adeline McConnico Kinnard. The original log church was replaced by a brick building which was destroyed by a tornado in 1909. The present building was then located on Liberty Pike. When McConnico performed the wedding ceremony of Emeline Wison to her cousin James Hazard Wilson II on March 21, 1821, the best mean was the eminent gentlemen, Sam Houston.

Besides McConnico and Watson, early family names include Hodge, Turner, Allen, and Williams. A Mr. Marshall, a Revolutionary War soldier, is buried on land now belonging to the J. F. Lynch family on Murfreesboro Road. The Lynches live in the home, a part of which was the Marshall home.

At one time, during this century, there was a country store in Mudsink run by Richard Smithson. A blacksmith shop stood near where Franklin East subdivision now stands. The nearest gristmill, schools, and churches were in Millview. An early mailman, Tyler Roscoe, carried the mail on motorcycle, and Leonard Britten was said to be the best of mail carriers. There was farming in the community and children liked to go rabbit hunting, fishing, and enjoyed being children when they weren't helping their parents.

While Mudsink was always small, never a full-fledged community, there is one reminder, the sign denoting the McConnico Meeting House, as a state historical marker. The marker was put up under the direction of the late Colonel Campbell Brown. While the flooding of Watson Creek gave Mudsink its name, it now has a bridge across the creek, and the name of Mudsink is merely a reminder on the map of Williamson County.

35

New Hope

THE COMMUNITY OF NEW HOPE, located west of Fairview, is part of a cluster effect. The map of Williamson County is full of many communities and a closer look shows that the western portion has more communities clustered in a small area than the southeastern portion. Why are communities like Bending Chestnut, Greenbrier, Liberty Hill, New Hope, and Craigfield crowded together in this part of Williamson County, while communities like Nolensville, Triune, and College Grove are spread out in the eastern part? This inconsistency is possibly because in the western portion travel was very difficult, with many mountain-like ridges and, at one time, roads ranged from poor to non-existent. So, wherever a gristmill, general store, or both, were set up, there was a community.

The country store was a necessity in such a rural community, and L. C. Richardson ran one store in New Hope. It was there residents purchased plow points and harness along with the staples they couldn't grow on their land. Richardson is remembered as a gentleman who was known and liked by everyone. Another store was run by Wash Brown. Mail first came to New Hope from the Jingo post office and an early postmaster was a Mr. Daubenspeck. The post office was located one mile east of John Griffin's farm.

The Church of Christ in New Hope was started around 1930, and was built on land donated by Leechie Buttrey. Consequently it became known as "Leechie's Church." Buttrey was also a school teacher and mail carrier. The Church of Christ is located on Highway 96, towards Dickson.

School at New Hope.

The school was located near Highway 96. It went through the eighth grade with students completing their education at Hillsboro. Lola Tidwell Overbey was one of the teachers, and Mrs. Kelly Arnold was at one time a cook who made sure the children had hot lunches during school.

One church building in the community saw several denominations before it was torn down to make room for a modern brick church. The

Methodist Church was started around 1900, and they used the building for thirty-five years. Then the Freewill Baptists took over for about five years. Later, the Missionary Baptists came in around 1946 and called it the Old New Hope Baptist Church. Soon the old building was leveled to make way for a brick church. John Lampley was pastor for twenty-three years, and he eventually branched out on his own to form the Old Path Baptist Church. Familiar family names like Daubenspeck, Lampley, Anderson, Richardson, Sullivan, Mangrum, and Buttrey all settled the New Hope community.

The gravel roads, Highway 96, Old Cox Pike, Crow Cut Road, and others were eked out with hard labor. Several men would hitch eight mules to a grader to make the road, and often these were young teenage boys as well as older men. Some roads, like Old Cox Pike, were tollroads. The tollgate was actually not a gate but really just a pole across the road. The toll was fifteen cents per wagon. The story is told about one old man who would come to the tollgate, then get out and start gnawing on the wagon spokes, making the gatekeeper think he was mentally incompetent. Of course he was fine, but the gatekeeper would let him through the tollgate without paying a fee.

There was also an Odd Fellows Lodge, one of the few in the county. The lodge members and their families would hold a celebration once a year, around the first of June, with dinner on the ground. It was a time of good food and fellowship. The Odd Fellows Lodge was one way the men had of working together to keep the community alive.

New Hope has three cemeteries, two on the north side of the Old New Hope Baptist Church, the other on the south side of the church. The area was good for cattle but only a few row crops. However, there was plenty of work in the woods.

An Autobiography of Albert Luther Daugherty was written for the author's own family to give people an idea what it was like to grow up and raise a family in a rural community. One paragraph talks about his getting married in 1925 and how he and his wife started life together:

> My wife went to a sale close (to Franklin), bought a glass door safe for 50¢ and bought a small cook stove for 75¢. The back of the stove between the fire and the bread made a big hole in it and ashes would fall in on the bread. We made out with the old stove over a year. I bought a new stove on a credit. I paid for it later.

> I must tell how much money we had when we got married.
> I had seven dollars and my wife had ten. But they were the
> good old days.

> I had two mules unbroke, and I had two or three hogs. My
> wife's parents gave her a cow that was giving milk, back in
> those days, milk and butter was half of your living.

In the portion of the book about his younger days he remembers raising sheep:

> I remember when I was about sixteen years old my dad raised
> sheep then. One day we put some wool in a large bag or sack.
> I went with two of our friends around twelve or fifteen miles
> to a carding mill to have the wool worked into rolls. We tied
> the bags behind the saddles. We rode, well I did a mule, and
> the other men rode horses.

> My mother spun the rolls and made thread and knit sox for
> the family. We raised cotton, picked the seed out of it and
> carded it, made rolls and then spun it into thread to knit sox
> out of it. My wife did a lot of work like this when we were
> raising our children. I'm still wearing some sox she knit for
> me years ago.

This little book is full of anecdotes about living in western Williamson County when life was simpler and, while it was more difficult, the family ties were close and the community was close. People who talk about New Hope say it has always been full of good neighbors who care about each other, which is what a community is all about.

———36———

Nolensville

COMMUNITY INCORPORATED IN 1838
NEAR MILL CREEK

T HE NOLENSVILLE COMMUNITY, started around 1800, grew and prospered, and in the 1930s, with the Nolensville Cooperative Creamery as a thriving industry, the town flourished. Several events, including the failure of the bank, destructive fires, and changing lifestyles, took their toll, but, like the Phoenix, Nolensville is again becoming a popular area in which to live outside the Metropolitan Nashville area. Now new stores, new homes, and new ideas are bringing the community back to life.

Nolensville, located in the eastern part of the county, was named for William Nolen whose home was built on nearby Mill Creek. Nolen came to the area from Virginia around 1797 when his family stopped in the wilderness area to repair a broken wagon wheel and found the location rich with good springs, good soil, and an abundance of wild game. The wilderness area, however, was so thick with canebrake, children had to wear bells around their necks to prevent them from getting lost or captured by the Indians. In 1810, John Wesley King, a Methodist minister, moved his family to Nolensville from North Carolina and helped found the Nolensville Methodist Church. The first water mill south of Nashville was built by Benjamin Kidd, giving Mill Creek its name.

An all-but-forgotten man in Tennessee history came from the Nolensville area and was the first native Tennessean ever to strive for the presidency of the United States. John Bell was born in the Mill Creek area (in Davidson County) of Nolensville Road on February 15, 1796, the son of Margaret and Samuel Bell. Bell went into law practice in Franklin and was later elected to the state senate from Williamson County. At the age of thirty, he defeated Felix Grundy for a congressional seat and served fourteen years in the House of Representatives. He later served in the United States Senate in 1847. In 1860, John Bell was candidate for president with the Constitutional Union Party, against Abraham Lincoln for the Republicans and Stephen Douglas for the Democrats. Bell carried only three states in the election—Tennessee, Kentucky, and Virginia, but did manage to carry his own county. That was the last of his political career and the short-lived Constitutional Union Party. Bell died in 1869.

Two Revolutionary War soldiers buried near Nolensville are Robert Osburn, who came to Williamson County in 1805 and died in 1834, and Richard C. Vernon, who moved here in the early 1800s and is buried near Nolensville.

Early religious gatherings in Nolensville were brush arbor meetings under the trees. At one time, a traveling Methodist minister borrowed a canoe from Timothy Demonbreun, early Nashville settler, paddled up Mill Creek to Antioch, left the boat, and walked the rest of the way to Nolensville.

The Nolensville community was incorporated in 1838, a year after the Mount Olivet Methodist Episcopal Church was organized. Thirty-seven members started the little church, and the organizing minister was probably Benjamin R. Gant. The first building was a log structure with a brick foundation, the bricks kilned right on the property. It was also used as an elementary school. A second building was constructed in 1853. In 1889, the church was part of the Nolensville Methodist Circuit, the other churches were at Triune and Hebron. A third church building was begun in 1894 on a new location to replace the second one which was in bad repair. Additions over the years included an iron fence, new stoves, and memorial windows as the congregation grew.

The Church of Christ was dedicated at Nolensville in 1893 by David Lipscomb. The Baptist church started out in 1951 as a mission church of the Concord Baptist Church, and most recently, a Cumberland Presbyterian church has been started, meeting first at the school, and land has been donated by the Jenkins family at York Road and Nolensville Road for the Cumberland Presbyterian church building.

Another early settler in the Nolensville community was Sherwood Green who came to the area as a member of a surveying crew. He built his home in a clearing one-half mile east of Nolensville on Rocky Fork Road,

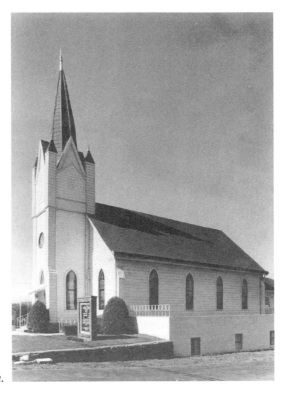

Nolensville Methodist Church.

and the home was built around 1800. As a surveyor, he often took payment for his work in land, soon acquiring thousands of acres in Williamson and Rutherford Counties.

Tradition has it that the first tobacco was raised in Nolensville by Byrd Hamlett and packed in hogsheads that had thorn pins driven in each end. Chains with rings in each end were hooked over the pins and carried by oxcart from Williamson County to the Cumberland River.

Benjamin King was operating the King's Inn on the Nolensville Turnpike in 1850, which later became the Nolensville Hotel. J. W. Williams operated it from 1892 until 1898. E. K. Hardison was another operator. A two-story log building with twelve rooms and a large lobby was on the Nolensville-Huntsville Turnpike, and the stagecoach stopped at the inn. Here travelers could change horses or rent horses and buggies. Many salesmen could stay at the hotel, rent a horse, and call on merchants in the area. The stagecoach stopped running in 1910.

William J. McMurray of Nolensville fought with the Twentieth Tennessee Regiment during the Civil War, then, after the war returned to Nolensville and graduated from the Nolensville Academy. He later studied and practiced medicine in Nashville.

Nolensville came into its own in the 1920s and 1930s with the coming of the Nolensville Cooperative Creamery in 1921. Nolensville was a big dairying community and, at one time, there were close to fourteen grade-A dairy farms on Rocky Fork Road alone. Mammoth Springs Dairy, the first grade-A dairy barn in the area, was run by Tom Scales, direct descendant of John Robertson of Nashville. The creamery employed enough people to keep it running all night long, with Walter York a chief buttermaker. Nolensville folk would buy the whey and buttermilk and feed it to their hogs, along with the grain. Workers would get paid by the creamery twice a month and the money would be spent at one of the many stores in Nolensville. They didn't need to travel to Franklin or Nashville for their supplies.

Four general stores were in Nolensville. They were run by J. B. Williams, W. J. Putnam, J. B. Osburn, and Emmett Williams. Grocers would make several trips a week to Nashville to stock up on supplies, rather than the usual weekly runs. An auto dealership was run by John Thomason; restaurants were owned and operated by Herbert Potts and Maw D. Williams. A barbershop was run by Ed House, and Joe Maxwell kept the horses and mules shod in his blacksmith shop. For many years, the livery stable stood across from the hotel and travelers would stable their horses there for the night. The concrete watering troughs at the hotel were a reminder of early days when the hotel was torn down in 1968. Ben Waller started the funeral home and the business is still in the family to this day. In fact, it is the oldest continuous family buisness in Williamson County. The Nolensville flour mill was right next to the creamery and children would slide down the wheat chute at the mill.

Several events changed the face of the community. The bank, which opened in 1906, failed in 1932, and it resulted in a severe financial loss to its customers. Major fires took their toll. The flour mill caught fire and burned for days. Another fire burned the livery stable, funeral home, post office building, and one of the stores.

The Nolensville Academy was a very early school in the area. There was a succession of several small-frame school buildings in the years to come. All too often, schools burned due to fires that were caused by overheated woodstoves. In 1938, the county bought land for a sturdier brick school with four rooms instead of one. While it was being constructed, students went to school in a tent. This school went through the tenth grade, then the students went on to Franklin or College Grove to finish their high school education. The boys loved to play basketball and had an outdoor basketball court. Going to College Grove or Franklin was a real treat since their basketball court was inside in the gym. After World War II, the people of the community got together to build a county gym. They were given permission to use materials from the mess hall at the army classification center on Thompson Lane, and the gym was constructed out of those materials.

One problem that recurred every year for many years was the problem of the water at the school. Each fall when the school opened, the children suddenly became ill. The water from the septic tank was seeping into the school's water system, but they didn't seem to be able to do anything about it. In the late 1960s, Nat Caldwell, a reporter for *The Tennessean* in Nashville, became aware of the problem and wrote a series of articles about it. The community, with the help of then Secretary of Agriculture Orville Freeman and Congressman William Anderson, was able to secure money from the Farmers' Home Administration for Nolensville's own water system.

Growing up in Nolensville, children loved to play in the creeks and hunt for arrowheads. They joined the 4-H Club, and when they won prize ribbons, it was a snip of blue, red, or white ribbon cut from a spool, rather than imprinted with gold letters as they are now. They marched in the Franklin Blue Ribbon parade in the 1930s if their teeth were sparkling and got a clean bill of health in the school checkups.

The Methodist church sponsored a basketball team and they played other churches. The recreation center had an excellent summer and winter program for the children, which is still going strong, and they had a lighted ball field for the children before the county recreation department was even begun.

The early post office was located on one side of W. J. Putnam's store and Miss Allie Pomeroy was a mail carrier. Dr. and Mrs. Dickey ran a drugstore, which was really just a small room to one side of Putnam's Store, where Dickey, (and he was not a medical doctor), dispensed medicines to those in need.

Early settlers and people who have made Nolensville prosper include the Nolen, Kidd, Green, King, Owen, Williams, Christmas, Chrisman, Gooch, McCord, Hall, Putnam, Jenkins, Scales, and Brittain families, to name just a few.

The community had a stockholders' telephone exchange in 1910 and when the main highway came through around 1930, the phone poles had to be moved. The road was built like many in the county, with horses, mules, pond scoops, and lots of manual labor.

Longtime Nolensville residents remember Tom Guthrie driving a spotted pony hitched to a spring wagon into town to get feed and stop at the creamery, Miss Nannie Williams coming sidesaddle on horseback, and Bill Williams driving a buggy with a gray mule hitched to it. When he got to the store he would sit around all day and smoke John Ruskin cigars.

The Nolensville community saw its best days before World War II. While the county built a new elementary school, it can be reminded of the days when four industrious ladies of the PTA, back in the 1930s, conducted bake sales, held horse shows, and were determined to raise enough money to buy land and help build the four-room brick school which was completed in 1938. These ladies were Mrs. Louise Williams, Mrs. Annis Osborne, Mrs. Ruth Williams, and Mrs. Elsie May Pickett.

The whole structure of life is changing; Nolensville is no longer a farming community. Its location, just two miles from Nashville, makes it convenient for subdivisions, and farm land is being sold in small tracts for homes. New businesses are springing up in locations away from the main part of town, but the town continues to grow and prosper, and the community feeling will always be part of Nolensville.

─── 37 ───

Peytonsville

ONCE CALLED
"SNATCHIT"

T HE COMMUNITY OF PEYTONSVILLE, located southeast of Franklin, has been known by three different names: Peytonsville, Little Texas, and Snatchit. In hard times, another name "Hungry" was given to the community. The name Peytonsville possibly came from some Peytons who settled in the area. The name Snatchit came about as a result of a ten dollar debt. In 1836, a creditor collected his due bill by snatching a ten dollar bill from the hand of the unsuspecting debtor, Andrew Campbell, hence the name Snatchit. After the Civil War, the community became known as Little Texas. Ex-Confederate soldiers, who were fugitives from justice, were forced to settle elsewhere. Many went to Texas where there was too much territory for the Union army to patrol. Others decided to hide out in the hills around Peytonsville. The area was full of family people who were clannish enough not to tell strangers if there was a fugitive in the area.

A very early settler to the area was John Secrest, a Revolutionary War soldier from North Carolina. He owned 381 acres of land in the county in 1816 and is buried in Peytonsville. According to the December 11, 1835, issue of the *Western Weekly Review,* Gibson and Cook opened a tanning establishment in the Peytonsville community, and they were paying in cash or leather for the hides.

One of the earliest buildings was that of the Cool Springs Primitive Baptist Church, built on the Arno-Peytonsville Road, by the big cool springs. Records of the church date back to 1818 and, in 1839, the church

141

was moved, log by log, by the congregation, up the hill to its present site, and, even though it's far removed from the actual springs, it is still called Cool Springs Church. In 1856, a committee was appointed to build a new meeting house, a frame building with two entrances, one for the men and one for the women, which was standard practice at the time. In 1873, the Cool Springs School was started, and the late Phil Bennett was one of the last surviving students at the Cool Springs School. Sunday, March 10, 1912, is remembered as one of the saddest days in the history of the church. Elder David Phillips, who had been preaching at the Cool Springs Church since 1893, began to feel ill during the services and stepped out of the pulpit. He asked Brother White to take his place. Phillips then sat down on one of the front pews and died at the age of sixty-one. The late Elder Milton Lillard, once pastor of the church, said his grandfather was in the congregation when this happened. The cemetery next to the church is on land donated by Mary Holland and was started near the turn of the century. The frame church was later bricked over and several rooms added.

The Peytonsville Methodist Church was started around 1857 and was at one time the oldest Methodist church in the conference until it became the Peytonsville Chapel of Hope in 1981. Will Stephens used to teach night singing school to both children and adults who wanted to improve their musical knowledge. The price was very reasonable, ten lessons for just one dollar, and during the winter months, they'd pull the organ around the coal stove to keep warm. The Masonic Lodge was located above the Methodist church, but when one of the many tornados which have done so much damage to the county ripped through the area, it tore off the top story of the church, and the Lodge was moved to Bethesda.

The first property owned by the Peytonsville Church of Christ was purchased on May 5, 1884, from C. W. Mallory and his wife. Trustees were James L. Gee, N. B. Vaden, and N. T. Smithson. The property was located about 300 yards out on Peytonsville Road and just on the opposite side of the road from the current church. Some of the ministers who preached at the early church were F. C. Sowell, Jim Dickson, Trice Dickson, Billy Brown, Lawrence Lewis, Billy Boyd, and J. T. Smithson. Leila Spear gave the property on which the present building stands, and the church was dedicated in the spring of 1951. In 1976, an additional acre of land was purchased from the Spear's estate. Some of the preachers in the present building include Silas Shaw, Ross Sanders, George Ryan, Charles Hicks, James Costello, and Leamon Flatt.

Vaden Smithson house.

The Peytonsville Baptist Church began as a mission church in a store building in August 1959. The mission church was sponsored by First Baptist Church of Old Hickory. The present structure was built in 1962.

Glenn's Store, on Peytonsville Road, was started around 1901 by the Mathis brothers. It had always been a store and there was once a barbershop attached. Marshall Warren bought the business in 1925 and he was unique as a store owner in that he was blind. He would weigh his own meat and make change for the customers, and he said he was never once cheated on by his customers. Warren was also a representative to the state legislature and Lonnie Ormes, state treasurer at the time, would drive him to the Hermitage Hotel during the legislative session. One day, Ormes decided to play a little trick on him. Instead of delivering him to the front door of the hotel, he pulled up at the rear entrance. Ormes said, "Here we are at the hotel." "Yes, I know," said Warren, "right at the back door." In 1937, the business was purchased by R. W. Glenn. Glenn was also the local magistrate and held Magistrate Court in the store.

During World War II, when so many foods were rationed, Peytonsville had three general stores, a cotton gin, a harness shop, and an overnight house for travelers heading down the main road to College Grove and Eagleville. A Mr. Frank drove a peddler's wagon through the community and before the turn of the century, there was a shop which sold buggies. Names of settlers and people who made Peytonsville grow include the Harrison, Southern, Gosey, King, Glenn, Bennett, and Hall families. The oldest house in the area is one built by Pettus Shelburne, now occupied by Billy Mangrum.

George Washington King gave land for the Peytonsville School, a two-room school which went through the eighth grade, and then students would complete their education in Franklin. In 1927, a junior high was added, bringing the school up through the tenth grade. Later, when the Bethesda School was built, Peytonsville reverted back to being an eight-grade school until it was no longer in use. Boys growing up in Peytonsville played baseball and basketball, no football, and challenged other communities. They even had a girls' basketball team which was tops in the county and part of the girls' uniform was a stylish pair of bloomers. Children's Day at the Methodist church meant recitals, singing, and dinner on the ground.

The nearest railroad station was at McDaniel, and relatives who would come to Peytonsville for summer church meetings could arrive at the McDaniel station, attend the festivities, then return home by train that night. Several famous people have gotten their start in Peytonsville. Sam and Kirk McGee of Grand Ole Opry fame and Tom Little, Pulitzer Prize winning cartoonist from *The Tennessean,* were all raised in this portion of Williamson County. Some good people and some good times have come from Peytonsville.

─── 38 ───

Riggs Crossroads

COMMUNITY SETTLED BY
RIGGS FAMILY

R IGGS CROSSROADS COMMUNITY is situated in the southeast corner of the Williamson County map and took its name from the Riggs family who settled there around 1810. Familiar names in the community like Ogilvie, Brittain, and Haley can trace their ancestry back to Edward Riggs, who was born in England in 1590 and came to America— Boston, Massachusetts, in 1633. His descendant, David Riggs, was the founder of the family who settled in Middle Tennessee. Early Riggs family members were translators of the Bible; one member settled among the Sioux Indians in the community of Lac-Qui-Parle in western Minnesota, and a later descendant was tennis great Bobby Riggs.

David Riggs was born in Morris County, New Jersey, in 1749, coming to Williamson County by way of North Carolina, in 1810. He and his wife had ten children, all of whom had moved to Williamson County by 1814. Tax records show that David Riggs paid taxes on 555 acres of land in 1811. In 1814 he was elected constable in Captain Hooker's company of militia. Before 1834, instead of civil districts, the county was divided into militia companies, and the county courts appointed a captain to be over each company. David Riggs and his son Gideon were instrumental in the establishment of Fishing Ford Road, now U.S. 31-A. It is the oldest traveled thoroughfare in Tennessee, even before Tennessee was a state, and it was a well-used trail for game. It was also used by northern and southern tribes of Indians in commerce and war. With the coming of settlers to the area, the Creek Indians used the trail for raids on the settlements. The first log house was built in the northwest corner of the crossroads and owned by

David Riggs. Later, Gideon lived there until he built his brick home. At least three other log houses were built on the property for tenants or slaves. As county tax records show, Gideon paid taxes on nine slaves in Tennessee.

Gideon Riggs, David's son, was a leader in the establishment of this community and at one time owned 1000 acres of land around the Crossroads area in Williamson, Marshall, and Rutherford Counties. Under his guidance, the homeplace grew to include six log houses, a brick home for himself, a post office, a blacksmith shop, and church. He lived until 1871 and, in spite of the financial devastation the Civil War brought southern land owners, he was able to leave a farm to each of his four children.

A stagecoach ran between Nashville and Chapel Hill with Riggs Crossroads a way station in the nineteenth century. A passenger could board the stage in what is now the Woodbine area of Nashville early in the morning, enjoy lunch at Nolensville for twenty-five cents, then arrive at Riggs Crossroads about five in the afternoon. The stagecoach was put out of business by the L & N Railroad around 1914.

In 1884, Thomas C. Brittain built a tobacco factory on the back of the property at Riggs Crossroads, and later his son Oliver Riggs Brittain added a tobacco warehouse. The business was later moved to Columbia, where it was ultimately bought by the American Tobacco Company.

The post office was established in 1834 and discontinued in 1872. Gideon Riggs was postmaster from 1834 until 1854 and again from 1866 until 1871. Between 1854 and 1866, his relatives served as postmaster. At its beginning, the post office was probably in Gideon's home as descendants remember seeing the letterbox fixtures in the old house. The blacksmith shop was situated in the southeast corner of the Crossroads and was torn down in the early 1900s. During the Civil War, Federal troops devastated the area of the Crossroads, as they did so many other places in southeast Williamson County. They burned rail fences, stole livestock, and managed to find and take hidden valuables.

The Riggs Crossroads Church of Christ began as a brush arbor meeting, but inclement weather was about to force cancellation of the meeting. Mr. Tatum, a rural mail carrier, contacted two denominational churches in the community about using their buildings to continue the meeting, but was refused. On returning home, he met Gideon Riggs, who was of no particular religious persuasion. Tatum told Riggs the situation, whereupon Riggs offered Tatum $100 and land on which to erect a church building. The offer was gratefully accepted, and the congregation met in the church building in May 1872, six months after the death of Gideon Riggs. Sunday school was started almost immediately and even though finances were scarce in 1888, they managed to send $13.25 to a mission church in Chattanooga. The lower level of the church was used as an elementary sub-scription school. After the church was forced to abandon the building because of the coming of the L & N Railroad tracks, Oliver Riggs Brittain, grandson of Gideon, deeded one acre of land on Horton Highway for the new church in 1911, where the church stands today.

The family cemetery at the Crossroads has managed to survive the coming of the highway and the railroad. It is reserved for and dedicated to the descendants of Gideon Riggs. Each Mother's Day, family members gather at the cemetery. A plaque honoring Gideon and his three wives has been placed at the entrance.

The construction of the L & N Railroad, completed in 1914, cut a large path through the middle of Gideon's farm, and the construction of U.S. Highway 31-A in the 1930s took another swipe at the farm. The Great Depression of the thirties caused many young people to leave the area and seek their fortunes elsewhere. The original farm has been divided into six parts and only three parts remain in the family. While drastic changes have come to the Crossroads, it is still a living, active community, and the descendants of David and Gideon proudly carry on the family name.

Cemetery at Riggs Crossroads.

39

Rudderville

CHILDREN IN RUDDERVILLE
ATTENDED ACCIDENT SCHOOL

WHILE THE RUDDERVILLE COMMUNITY, on Arno Road, had a school appropriately called the Rudderville School, the first facility for educating the youngsters was called Accident. It was situated on the Bill May property, towards Arno. How or why it got its name, no one knows. Alice Pollard was a teacher at Accident School when she was eighteen years old; Kate Waddey was another. Other teachers in the Rudderville community were Kate Cotton Hatcher, Miss Anna Neeley, Gene Graves, and Miss Allie Wilson, who is remembered for the hot soup she would cook on the potbellied stove. The school later became known as Sunnyside School, because no one was too fond of the unusual name Accident School. The Rudderville School was started as a one-room schoolhouse, with two rooms added later. The school educated youngsters in the area until it closed in 1942. When children walked or rode their ponies to school, there was a shed attached to the school so the animals could stay out of the elements while the children learned their ABCs. Two teachers at the Rudderville School were Vivian Grigsby and Mary White. This school took the place of the Accident School about 1923.

The Rudderville community was originally a Revolutionary War land grant given to a Colonel Starnes, whose wife's maiden name was "Rudder," hence the name, Rudderville. The most prominent early landowners were the Starnes and Patton families, owning most of the land from Rudderville to Millview. A Revolutionary War soldier, Henry Sledge, came to this area from Virginia and is buried at Rudderville.

Rudderville never had its own church so people attended the Wesley Chapel Church at Arno or the Epworth Methodist Church at Millview. But there was a gristmill, sawmill, feed mill, blacksmith shop, and general store. The blacksmith shop near the store was run by Jim Will Culberson, who also ran the gristmill and feed mill.

J. N. Akin and S. A. Smithson bought the general store from the original owners in 1906. S. A. Smithson ran the business for fifty-five years. Then it was run by Van Smithson, followed by Howard Smithson, who bought the store and the house nearby and ran the store for twenty-three years. Before the days of large department stores, the Rudderville Store carried hardware, clothes, and plow points, in addition to groceries.

Electricity came to Rudderville around 1940; before that, ice for cooling was brought from Franklin. Three-hundred-pound blocks of ice were stored in the sawdust in an icehouse next to the store. A good portion of this ice was sold over a weekend.

A store run by Walter Smith and Louis Parrish later became Robert White's feed mill. Robert and Jimmy White bought the store around 1960 and added the mill, now closed, about 1965.

Rudderville Store, 1985.

Like many communities, the Rudderville boys had their baseball and basketball teams, playing other communities in weekend games. Les Stephens, who owned property where the Page Middle School now sits, had the first car in Rudderville, and people traveling from Rudderville to Franklin considered it a two- or three-patch road. It was so bumpy the tires would blow out several times en route, necessitating a pump and patches for the tires on any journey, long or short. There were no mechanics for emergency repair services.

Other families in addition to Starnes, Pollard, and Smithson responsible for settling Rudderville include the Akin, Johnston, Noland, Parrish, Pinkston, Crunk, Graves, Crafton, Stevens, and Harper families. The Luster family has also owned property in Rudderville for many years. While Rudderville, still unincorporated, has never been a large community, some of the same families have lived there for years and will continue to do so. Newcomers are arriving in the area, which now has both Page High and Page Middle Schools, and the Arno, Millview, Peytonsville, and Rudderville area is slowly growing.

40

Southall

SHALE ROCK ONCE MINED
AT SOUTHALL

T HE QUIET COMMUNITY OF SOUTHALL, located just off Carter's
Creek Pike, was once the scene of an incident which could have
started a small war right in Franklin. In 1868, just three years after
the Civil War, a young girl in Southall was attacked by a black man, who
was later apprehended. He was taken to jail in Franklin, and later removed
from the jail, carried four miles out of town, and shot. The next day, sup-
posedly in retaliation for the killing, fifty to seventy-five people, both black
and white, ambushed some young men walking from Franklin to Southall,
among them, the girl's twenty-year-old brother, who was killed in the incident. Word of the attack on the young girl and the ambush attack on her
brother spread to Nashville by way of train travelers, and the incident was
recorded in the *Nashville Union* and *American* papers. There were also
reports that all of Franklin was arming against possible riots. Measures
were taken for self-protection and the town was guarded all night. While no
major incidents occurred, the community was on edge, but evidently,
calmer heads prevailed and things soon returned to normal.

Records show that in 1814, John Southall, who had come to
Williamson County with his wife and mother, was buying land in what is
now the Southall community. The Southall property ran from Blazer Lane
to Hillsboro Road to Beard's Store, at the crossroads. James Southall lived
in the community in the early 1800s and his home was used as a voting
place in 1836, for the county's Fifth District.

The Berea Church of Christ, still going strong in the community, was

151

started in the year of our country's centennial, 1876. The church grew out of a meeting conducted by a Brother Elam. The original frame building is still used today, but the original front, with the two doors, one entrance for men, one for women, has been modernized with a single door. The church has, over the years, added Sunday school rooms, a nursery, a vestibule, and a baptistry. The late Glen Overbey was a Sunday school teacher at the church for more than thirty years and was also the church treasurer.

Berea Church of Christ.

The White's Chapel Methodist Church was situated across the road from the Church of Christ. It has been out of existence for many years, the congregation now worshiping at Methodist churches in Franklin.

In 1905, Jim Andrews operated a store at the crossroads when J. W. Yates moved his family from the Garrison community to open another store in Southall. Yates had operated a store in Garrison but decided to move when the stave mill closed down at Garrison. He operated the Southall Store for thirty years; the business later was owned by his wife Carrie, and his daughter, Miss Chloe Yates. While he managed the store, he also ran a peddler's wagon, going to neighbors and buying chickens, hams, and fresh produce to trade in Nashville for grocery items. The Southall blacksmith shop was run for many years by Pete Scruggs.

The Southall School was a one-room, eight-grade school. One outstanding teacher was Mrs. B. W. Worley. She was tall and slender and she has been described as a "female Ichabod Crane," but the description was given with affection by the only ninth-grade pupil she ever taught. She normally taught sixty students, grades one through eight, but the year it was time for W. C. Yates to leave the Southall School for Franklin High School, (his older sister was already at Franklin High), J. W. Yates didn't feel he could afford to clothe two growing youngsters who both attended the high school. So Mrs. Worley volunteered to teach the younger Yates at the school. She must have done well because by the time he graduated from Franklin High, he was the class salutatorian, and to this day, has left his mark on education in Williamson County. Mrs. Worley was an industrious lady who walked the two miles to and from school each day. Her daughter went on to become the first special education teacher in the Nashville City school system, and her son became a vice president with South Central Bell. Her husband ran a blacksmith shop two miles from Southall.

The Southall School was located on top of a rocky hill and during the warm weather little boys would go barefoot, and it was not an uncommon sight to see many toes bandaged from the sharp rocks around the school yard. At school, the children played baseball and the boys liked to go cane hunting. They would find a properly sized piece of cane, make a round ball out of clay, and spear the clay on top of the cane. They would whip the ball out of sight so that when it hit a nearby metal roof, the noise resounded loudly.

When Fred J. Page was Williamson County school superintendent, he made sure all the schools in his jurisdiction were open eight months of the year, which was not the case in all counties. He also traveled by horse and buggy to all his schools, giving speeches to the children, and in schools in outlying areas, he would make arrangements to stay overnight at one of the nearby homes. At county schools, like Southall, each teacher was responsible for the education in their school, and they would get together at teachers' meetings and swap books.

Mac and Will Southall ran a lumber company with offices in both Hillsboro and Franklin. The Middle Tennessee Railroad, a log hauling and phosphate line with an engine and two passenger cars, ran through the Southall community right behind the Yates' home. In fact, it ran through the backyard, between the house and the barn. When Claude Yates was going to high school, he took the train to and from Franklin. Coming home in the afternoon, he would wave to his family on the back porch as he passed by, then get off at the next stop and hike the mile back home. Boys liked to take horseshoe nails, put them on the train tracks and make the flattened nails into rings.

J. W. Yates purchased his first automobile in 1921, a Ford Model T touring car. The car was purchased from Bob Jennings at J. M. King's auto dealership on Franklin's town square. When Jennings sold the car to Yates, he also had to teach him to drive, and drive they did. On his first attempt behind the wheel, the car left the road and managed to straddle a barbed wire fence. Yates, Jennings, and the car went down the fence line with Yates in the driver's seat hollering "Whoa! Whoa!" When he did learn to drive, J. W. Yates and his family would attend services at a church in Garrison and cause quite a sensation since it was the only car there and the horses would become disturbed.

The Southall Home Demonstration Club was started in the 1930s by Mrs. J. D. King Sr. when Virginia Carson Jefferson was the Home Demonstration agent. Mrs. Jefferson conducted the programs at all the meetings, and would even come to individual's houses to cull chickens for them.

During World War II, the Home Demonstration agent set up cooperative canning clinics where each club would have a day set aside in the summer to can produce for the winter months. Once a year, Home Demonstration Clubs would hold a club rally, where the participants dressed in white and held a parade down Main Street in Franklin.

In the 1930s, shale rock was mined in Southall, and the shale was turned into a fine powder which was used as pigment in paint and mortar. During World War II, war bond drives were taking place all over the county, and in Southall, Glen Overbey and Jim Cannon were head of their drive and always managed to go over their quota of bonds sold.

Some names who have settled in the Southall community are Ballard, Ormes, Baxter, Coleman, Cook, Sparkman, Sawyer, Lillie, and Kinnard, to name just a few. Familiar sights in the town were those of Will Ladd, who managed a large farm nearby, driving thirty mule teams loaded with wheat to Nashville, or a thousand head of sheep being driven on foot through the town on their way to Franklin for shipment to market.

Claude Yates has said a community is made up of institutions and the people they serve. Southall had two churches, two stores, and a blacksmith shop, and it reached out into the lives of many. Southall was and is a versatile community.

─────── 41 ───────

Thompson Station

SITE OF CIVIL WAR BATTLE
MARCH 1863

THE COMMUNITY OF THOMPSON STATION, ten miles south of Franklin on Highway 31, was the site of a Civil War battle, a successful railroad shipping center, home of a broom factory, and a bank once prospered in the community. The town was named for the man who gave the land for the town, Dr. Elijah Thompson, but one of the earliest settlers was Francis Giddens, a Revolutionary War soldier who came to the area around 1800. His home, built in 1819, stands on the west side of Columbia Pike and was once the manor house in the Thompson Station area. Today, known as Homestead Manor, it is owned by Dr. and Mrs. William J. Darby, who have restored it to a home of charm and dignity.

Francis Giddens' first home was a log cabin on Murfree Creek, where he lived until his home was completed. He was also proprietor of the first licensed establishment in the area, a tavern called "Giddens," where he was owner, proprietor, and "keeper of the mail." In August 1801, the Williamson County Court ordered Francis Giddens along with six others to lay out the first road in the Thompson Station area. Later in 1832, the charter for Columbia Pike was granted.

The man for whom the town was named, Elijah Thompson, was engaged in cotton speculation, farming, and he was also a surgeon during the Civil War. He later served two terms in the Tennessee General Assembly, 1839 to 1841 and 1849 to 1851. One of Dr. Thompson's daughters, Alice, was a heroine of the Battle of Thompson Station. The battle took place in March 1863, many months before the Battle of Franklin in November 1864.

Alice Thompson, age seventeen, left her home before the fighting and took refuge in the cellar of Homestead Manor. After nearly five hours of fighting, she saw the color bearer fall. Running from her hiding place, she picked up the colors and waved them over her head, shouting encouragement to the troops. While waving the flag, a bombshell fell at her feet but failed to explode. Later she tore up her skirt to bind the soldiers' wounds.

The Battle of Thompson Station was a battle of the cavalry, with the Confederates eventually victorious, but it was considered a hollow victory as the village was untenable for future operations. Among the soldiers serving with General Nathan Bedford Forrest for the Confederacy was sixteen-year-old Newton Cannon, grandson of Newton Cannon of Kirkland, first governor of the state from Williamson County. Young Cannon enlisted in May 1862, one month before his sixteenth birthday. In 1922, Cannon wrote his reminiscences and told of his part in the battle at Thompson Station: "We captured twenty-two hundred of his (the Federal leaders') men after a hard fight at Thompson Station, fighting dismounted. I had my spur and boot-heel shot off. The wide-bossed spur saved my ankle. I was carried off the field, but soon returned to the line as I got use of my leg and stayed until they surrendered" (*The Reminiscences of Newton Cannon, First Sergeant, C.S.A.*, © 1963 by Samuel M. Fleming Jr.). After the battle, in May of that same year, Maj. Gen. Earl Van Dorn, leader of the Confederate troops along with Forrest, was assassinated in Spring Hill by Dr. George B. Peters, with whose wife Van Dorn had been keeping company. The doctor later divorced his wife, saying they had been separated since May 1, 1863, a month before Van Dorn's death. His obituary was hidden in the newspapers, as it was the same week General Stonewall Jackson died.

Before the war, in 1860, Thompson Station was already on the Tennessee & Alabama Railroad line, and the Louisville & Nashville became part of the system in 1862. As a result of the railroad, Thompson Station was a very successful shipping center, with farmers driving their hogs, cattle, and sheep down public roads to the rail line. Farmers also shipped grain by the carload, becoming the German millet seed market of the world. At the railroad office, there was a telegraph system and freight office.

The post office was located just a few feet away and the railroad built a walk from the tracks to the post office. Residents got their mail once a week at the post office, before mail was delivered by rural routes. Some early rural mail carriers in Thompson Station were James Washington Beasley, Edgar Hatcher, a Mr. Cowles, M. E. Montgomery, Will Mefford, and Clayton Arnold.

Arnold left a sizeable sum of his earnings to the University of Tennessee.

In the late 1800s and early part of this century, there was a very active blacksmith shop for horses and mules. There were several granaries and when Thompson Station was the end of the railway line, seven or eight saloons thrived. The home of Mrs. Dorothy Lea on Columbia Pike was a tavern in the days when the stagecoach traveled through the community. In the early 1900s, Thompson Station had a broom factory which employed a number of local people and was owned by Milton C. Hatcher. The factory burned and the operation was moved to Memphis, but Thompson Station area farmers continued to grow broom corn to ship to Memphis.

The Thompson Station Bank and Trust Company was built in 1913 on Thompson Station Road in the center of town. C. B. Alexander headed the bank. One day, before 1920, T. H. (Daddy) Timmons took a wheelbarrow to the bank and told Alexander he wanted to withdraw all of his cash, a grand total of $10,000. Alexander gave him the money, which was put into the wheelbarrow. Timmons headed home, while Alexander made a hasty trip to Franklin to replenish his depleted supply of cash. The very next day, Alexander was surprised to see Timmons returning with all the money.

Thompson Station Bank.

Timmons said he merely wanted to see if it was all there. The bank closed in 1927 and the building, still standing, was later used as a private home.

One of the earliest churches in the county was the Thompson Station Church of Christ, founded around 1845 with fifteen members. The original white-frame building is still in use, although as with most country churches, it was originally built with separate entrances for men and women. In the early days, baptizing was done in Cannon's Creek or under the trees near the bridge just north of Spring Hill, and later at baptistries at sister churches. A baptistry was not built until 1961 at the church. The church was also used as a hospital during the Battle of Thompson Station, and bullet marks were made on the front walls during the battle, the bullets staying in the building until they were removed in the mid-1970s.

Dr. Hiram Laws, who married Mary Thompson, daughter of Dr. Elijah Thompson, founded the Thompson Station Methodist Church in 1873. Members of the congregation first met at the Thompson Station Church of Christ and later at the school. The church was first organized with sixteen members drawn from the Spring Hill, Cowles Chapel, and Pope's Chapel Churches. The sanctuary of the present church was completed in 1876 and the building first called Wilkes Chapel for the Reverend P. C. Wilkes, leader of the congregation. The name was later changed to Thompson Station.

At one time there were four schools in the community: one on the Thompson Station-Burwood Road; another, a one-room log structure, on a hill above the Church of Christ; one on Critz Lane; and the other, for the black children, on Connection Hill. The Thompson Station Home Demonstration Club, first organized in 1926, was an energetic group of ladies who took it upon themselves to sponsor a hot lunch program for the school before the coming of the government-sponsored program. In 1945, this same group managed to have the old West Harpeth School moved from the West Harpeth community to Thompson Station to become a meeting place for the organization. The building was renovated and later moved a second time, to be used as a guest house behind Homestead Manor, the home of Dr. and Mrs. William Darby.

Numerous black families made contributions to the Thompson Station community, many working on farms and in the homes. Some black families who have been a part of the community for many years include the Norths, Fitzgeralds, McKissacks, Pattons, Longs, Browns, Nevils, Johnsons, Steeles, and Ridleys.

Early doctors include Dr. John Gillem Clay, Dr. W. W. Graham, Dr. J. W. Greer, Dr. W. H Arnold, and Dr. Gibbs, a dentist. Dr. Clay began his practice at Thompson Station in 1882, and one story concerning Dr. Clay is that he attempted to court, unsuccessfully, one of the widows of the community. Failing this, he married a lady who insisted on calling him "precious," and he became known as "Mr. Precious."

Tennessee Livestock Producers, an affiliate of the Tennessee Farm Bureau, was started in 1956 under the name Nichols Brothers, by Tom and the late Joe Nichols.

The charm and hospitality of Thompson Station has continued through the years of growth and change, and changes coming in the near future promise to be dramatic. The people of Thompson Station are determined to hold onto their way of life and have formed the Thompson Station Community Association to ease the transition from the quiet community of the past, to what may become a more bustling community in the future.

42

Trinity

COMMUNITY'S FIRST PUBLIC SCHOOL
ATOP METHODIST CHURCH

THE COMMUNITY OF TRINITY, located on Wilson Pike between Clovercroft and Nolensville, is an area of beautiful homes and two historic churches. The present school was the second consolidated school in the county, Lipscomb Elementary School being the first. One of the early buildings in the community was the Methodist Episcopal Church, now known as Trinity Methodist Church. It was first built on Burke Hollow Road and called Mount Zion. In 1863, during the Civil War, Federal troops came through the area, completely wrecked the building, and carried the materials off to Daddy's Knob, located directly behind the church. After the war, the congregation pitched in and began to rebuild. They bought two and one-half acres of land from Thomas Walkup Cunningham for about $100 per acre. Bricks for the church were made by hand by William M. McMahon, and after almost four years of hard work, a two-story brick structure on Wilson Pike was ready for occupancy. The congregation made the most of the building by putting two rooms upstairs, using the large room for a school and the smaller one for the Masonic Hall. The church had a seating capacity of about 300 people. First pastor of the church was A. F. Lawrence. From the close of the war until the church was completed, the congregation had been worshiping in empty houses.

By 1881, the Sunday school at Trinity Church had seventy-eight members, but from 1879 until 1887, Sunday school was suspended during the winter months because of the cold. When the Women's Missionary Society was organized in 1884, they met during the spring and summer months only. In 1897, tragedy struck when a tornado wrecked the church, and in 1909, another tornado blew out the north and east sides of the building. After each tornado, the congregation, undaunted, stayed together and worshiped in the vacant storehouse at Rock Hill. In 1907, the church finally received money from the federal government which had been due them for over forty years. The government paid them $1100 for damages done to the Mount Zion Church in 1863 during the Civil War, and this money was applied to the building of the parsonage. Changes have occurred over the years, such as the adding of a new Sunday school annex in 1956, a new parsonage in 1961, and members shared their building with members of the Lutheran faith while St. Andrew's Lutheran Church was being constructed.

The other church in Trinity is the Jones Chapel Church of Christ, which started with a tent meeting around 1880, when S. M. Jones was the preacher. Before a church building was constructed they met in members' homes. The tornado which hit Trinity Methodist also blew away Jones Chapel. It was rebuilt and a second time it too was hit by a tornado. The present church is the third building.

In 1883, several prominent people in the Trinity community applied for a charter to start the Trinity Academy. They wanted an institute of learning which would confer degrees, have a debating society, historical society, and library, and promote the fine arts. The charter was granted in May of 1883, but it is not known if the school was successful.

The Trinity School, on Wilson Pike, was the third school in the community. It was the second consolidated school under the Williamson County School Board. When Trinity area consolidated about 1947, it was made up of the following community schools: Arrington, Warren, Millview, Gooch, Split Log, and Trinity. Change always brings concern and complaints, and this was no exception. Everyone wanted the new consolidated school built in their area and there were a lot of upset folks before things settled down and people got used to having one school do the work of many. The first public school was on top of the Trinity Methodist Church. The second school was built on Wilson Pike and at one time went through all twelve grades. When the community decided to simply make it an eight-grade school, high school students went on to Franklin or took the train over to College Grove. The present school on Trinity Road was opened in 1991.

Doctors in the Trinity community included Dr. Rufus Crockett and his brother, Dr. John B. Crockett. Dr. Rufus Crockett lived near the Trinity

Trinity Methodist Church.

Methodist Church. Prominent families in the area included the Crockett, Lytle, Peebles, Pollard, Whitfield, Fly, Wilson, Herbert, Tulloss, Jordan, and McMahon families.

One of several beautiful, old homes in the Trinity area is called Inglehame. It was built before the Civil War by James Hazard Wilson II and was given the name Harpeth for the headwaters of the Little Harpeth River which ran nearby. The home burned in 1938 while undergoing remodeling by the owners Mr. and Mrs. Vernon Sharp, but was rebuilt, using the original exterior walls. The owners moved back in in 1940.

There was a blacksmith shop in the community, and two stores, one at Burke Hollow Road and one across the street from the railroad tracks, both run by people named Lamb. Mail was gathered at Arrington or Franklin and people could get their mail from the post office at Rock Hill.

The Trinity area, like all of Williamson County, is growing, but a drive down beautiful Wilson Pike reveals the many magnificent homes of the past which have added so much to the surroundings.

43

Triune

A PROSPEROUS COMMUNITY
BEFORE THE CIVIL WAR

THE COMMUNITY OF TRIUNE, once called Hardeman Cross Roads, was the home of a female Confederate spy, had its own newspaper, was the scene of a genteel southern dance during the midst of the Civil War, and site of five brick school buildings built between 1820 and 1845. Before 1860, Triune was recognized as a center of wealth, education, and culture.

One of the first settlers was Maj. John M. Nelson, a Revolutionary War soldier who came to the Triune area about 1785 and formed the town of Nelsonville. Nelson Creek also takes its name from Maj. Nelson. Nelsonville was laid out in tracts of half-acre and ten-acre lots. The half-acre lots sold for ten dollars each, the ten-acre tracts selling at thirty dollars apiece with provisions that they have homes on them within two years. He sold about thirty lots to settlers and the rest to Newton Cannon of Kirkland.

Another early settler was William Jordan, a Revolutionary War soldier from Virginia, who purchased 500 acres near Triune in 1796. He and his ten grown sons built numerous homes in the area.

Bailey Hardeman, early planter and merchant in the area, had a license-operated "ordinary" or tavern as early as 1802. Flemingsburg, about a mile east of Triune, was the site of a thriving community of stores, a tailor's shop, harness shop, and undertaking establishment. Tradition has it that it was destroyed by fire before the Civil War.

One of the highest spots in Triune is Sumner's Knob, where it is said on a clear day and with a good set of binoculars, one can see the courthouse

164

clock on the Rutherford County Courthouse. Sumner's Knob was property given to General Jethro Sumner as a Revolutionary War grant but was tended by his son Thomas Edward Sumner. The highest point on the property was used as a burial ground for early settlers such as Beasley, Peay, Russwurm, Clark, Jarrett, and Martin, among others.

John S. Russwurm, whose home was on the Spanntown Road, unknowingly captured the famous highwayman John Murrell on Russwurm's property and rode with him into Franklin. Only when Russwurm reached Franklin did he realize whom he had captured and was surprised he made the trip alive.

The magnificent antebellum home "Westview" belonging to Samuel Perkins was the site of a grand ball, in the tradition of the old South, right in the middle of the war. In December 1862, young gentlemen of the Confederacy danced until 4 A.M., then two hours later were in the midst of battle. On the farm of Hartwell Hyde, Federal soldiers were imprisoned in the smokehouse with grates over the windows to prevent their escape. The John Jordan home, which was actually built by Thomas Porter, was the home of Miss Mary Overall, a southern beauty who charmed Federal officers and was able to get military information from them. There is a strong possibility that young Sam Davis, who was captured in 1863, had papers on him which had been given him by Mary Overall, but he never betrayed his informer when he went to his death.

Of the five schools built between 1820 and 1845 in Triune, the first was Harpeth Union Male Academy. The Hardeman Academy, a boarding school for boys, was opened around 1828 and ran until it closed before the Civil War. It reopened in 1865 with education for both boys and girls. The Arrington Academy was built on the Page plantation and used by both sexes. The Triune Female Academy, known as Porter's Female College, was destroyed by the Federals in 1863, but the federal government paid back half the cost of the school in 1907. There was also a Harpeth Female Academy in Triune. The Bostick Female Academy was started as a girls' school with money left in the will of a wealthy Triune citizen. The school, situated high on a hill overlooking Horton Highway, was started in 1885 as a liberal arts school with as many as seventy-five students including boarding students.

In 1860, Williamson County was third in the state in terms of wealth, with Triune the richest district in the county. At that time, there were five general stores, a tailor's shop, saloon, shoe shop, undertaker, blacksmith, woodworking shop, carriage shop, two doctors, and even a weekly

Bostick Female Academy, later Triune School.

newspaper (one source says it was called the *Gazette*, another, the *Eclipse*).

When the question of secession came up in 1861, the Triune citizens voted against it. But when Abraham Lincoln called for volunteers to invade the South, they changed their minds and immediately two companies were formed. One was led by Thomas Benton Smith from Triune, who was to become a brigadier general before his twenty-fifth birthday. Another company was named Webb Company for Dr. Webb, who lived between College Grove and Triune. This company was made up of men from the College Grove, Triune, and Peytonsville areas.

Triune was the scene of two battles and thirteen skirmishes between December 1862 and February 1865. One incident occurred in 1862 when a Federal wagon train and 150 prisoners were captured. It was loaded with plunder from area farms. The corn, poultry, clothing, and other items were removed, and the 150 prisoners forced to ride mules bareback towards Murfreesboro. The Civil War devastated Triune. Few families were untouched by tragedy and it was said that by 1865, a man could ride cross country, between Triune and Nashville without a single fence standing in his way.

Two churches are prominent in the history of Triune. The Triune Methodist Church started out as a log building southeast of the present location, called King's Chapel. It was built in 1815 and at nearby King's Campground, large outdoor meetings were held by outstanding ministers of the day. In 1840 the church was moved to its present location, but even though the congregation worshiped in the building, the church was not officially dedicated until 1849, when all the debts were paid. The name Triune was given to the church by Reverend McFerrin at this time, and the community, known as Hardeman Cross Roads, also adopted the Triune name. In 1863, Federal troops burned the church, but was it rebuilt on the same foundation in 1866 and dedicated in 1872. Payment for damages done during the war finally came in 1907. The Masonic Lodge was located on the second story, and the cemetery was in the churchyard. It now goes around three sides of the church and there are still gravesites available. The United Methodist Women was organized at the Triune Church in 1878 by Jane Lytle King, who also planted the pine trees around the church, one of which is still standing. She also gave the Communion silver to the church. In 1878, the women also sent a pledge to Lochie Rankin, the first missionary to China. Additions to make the church in the shape of a cross were added in 1956, and the church is still growing today.

The Wilson Creek Meeting House, a Primitive Baptist church, was started in 1804 from members in Garner McConnico's Big Harpeth Baptist Church. The building, constructed in 1815, is believed to be the oldest church building in the county. During the Civil War, the church was used as a prison by Union soldiers. Rebel soldiers who were considered troublemakers were kept in the basement. Names and regiments carved in the white pillars supporting the building are still visible. The church was used in World War I for happier gatherings. The ladies would hold quilting bees and make wrapped bandages for the servicemen. It was the only church in which the benches could be pushed back against the wall to hold the quilting frames.

Telephone service came in 1907 and the switchboard, delivered by wagon from New York to Holton Adam's store in Triune, served twenty-six customers at first. Dial service came in 1955.

Puckett's Grocery, one store in Triune started in 1913, is still in operation. John Watson Puckett converted an old granary into a general store and it stayed in his family, through growth and expansion, for sixty-six years. It has been a Triune gathering place for over sixty years.

The old Bostick Female Academy was used as a public school from 1900 until 1947 and went from first grade through high school. It was also used as a community club, a Home Demonstration Club meeting place, and a voting precinct. Today it is a private home.

Triune is not the wealthy community it once was, but its history is preserved in the many beautiful homes, and a trip up Sumner's Knob reveals the names of the courageous and adventurous pioneer settlers who moved to the Triune community so long ago.

44

West Harpeth

COMMUNITY ONCE SHIPPED 2400 LAMBS
TO THE EAST COAST

THE COMMUNITY OF WEST HARPETH is situated just off Columbia Pike, south of Franklin, and along the West Harpeth River, from which it took its name. The community grew up around the L & N Railway tracks and the West Harpeth Depot. There were two general stores, a large granary (called a warehouse), two blacksmith shops, a prominent doctor, a school, and a church.

Before the community began to grow, a beautiful home called the Willows was constructed by John Watson, who settled in the county around 1800. The bricks for the dwelling were made on the property. A mile-long race track ran in front of the house and John Watson and his friends enjoyed the gentlemanly sport of horseracing. The home was later rented by the Critz family, who occupied the home when the tornado of 1920 went through the community. Mrs. Critz managed to shelter her children from the tornadic winds, but the house was almost destroyed and the outbuildings lost. For three months the family lived in tents in the yard and rebuilt the two-story house, this time, with only one story. The house is currently owned by C. D. Berry III, whose grandfather, C. D. Berry, had purchased the property in 1892.

Other early settlers include Tristram Patton and Jordan Reese. Reese, while living in Virginia, bought property in West Harpeth for his son-in-law. Other early families were the Norths, Dudleys, and Stokes. But before these settlers, there were Indians in the area. One man, Henry North, while

169

farming, plowed up an Indian skeleton, took it home, and put it under his bed. However, when he later married, his wife probably made haste to get rid of it.

The West Harpeth School and the Bethel Methodist Church were built just a few feet from each other. The school went through the eighth grade and the children had to carry water from the creek—two children on either side and a broom handle with a bucket between them. They had to walk the footlog across the creek to get the water back to the school. At least fifteen children had to be enrolled in the small school for classes to be held. With only one teacher, the older students would help the younger ones with their lessons. Some of the early teachers were Vashti Early, Myrtle Thweatt Jordan, Beulah Green, and Cleo Grigsby.

The building itself was constructed around 1900 and moved to Thompson Station for use by the ladies' Home Demonstration Club in 1945. It is still standing, having been refurbished as a guest house on private property, in the Thompson Station area.

The Bethel Methodist Church, also built around the mid-1800s, was a brick building. It was a member of the Methodist Episcopal Church, South. One Sunday, when the church was having a special dinner on the ground after Sunday morning services, one parishioner, Thunie Cunningham, decided the preacher was becoming too long-winded. She left the building, went to her car, lay on the car horn, and in two minutes, the church emptied. The preacher had gotten the message.

April 20, 1920, was a memorable day for the community when a tornado ripped through the area. The school teacher had to make a hasty decision whether to take the children from the school over to the church next door, where she felt they might be safer, or keep them with her at the school. She decided to move them to the church, and ironically, it was the church building which was completely destroyed. Four boys left the school and took refuge in a building used to store coal located just behind the church. When they saw the bricks fly off the church, they got out of the building and then began helping the teacher get the children out of the demolished church and back to the school by edging their way along a fence. Damage done to the school was limited to the loss of the porch and roof and, fortunately, there were no serious injuries to the children.

The West Harpeth community, which grew up along the railroad, had a granary, a large long building which is still standing with holding pens underneath. The granary stored wheat and the pens were used for lambs

A West Harpeth general store.

later taken by train to market. One year, 2400 lambs were shipped off, one of the largest orders going to Jersey City, New Jersey. Very little cattle were shipped since sheep could be fattened on grass alone. Today, the county's lamb population has decreased with the coming of so many subdivisions and numerous dogs. Along with the wheat, corn and millet were also shipped from the West Harpeth granary, the corn being stored in a corn-crib in back.

Two stores served the community, one, a large building still standing across the road from the granary, was first owned by Chapman Anderson and later John Jordan. Jordan also served as postmaster for West Harpeth when he ran the store. Jordan left the business in 1918 to work for the Harpeth National Bank in Franklin, later becoming president of the bank. He left Harpeth National Bank in the 1940s to accept a position as post-master at Franklin. The store was later run by Emmett Pollard who also ran the post office, located in the same building. The telegraph office was located at the depot. The other store, situated at a fork in the West Harpeth Road, was run by Lawrence Horton. The North family had a flour mill on the river, and there were two blacksmith shops, one run by a Johnson, the other by Andrew Forsythe.

The big event of the summer in West Harpeth was the community picnic on the spacious front lawn of the Cunningham farm. The Cunninghams would stretch fence wire, laid flat between two trees, and the community would turn it into a groaning board, laden with some of the best food around. One year, Governor Henry Horton lent his presence to the picnic.

Dr. J. W. Greer, the community physician, lived in the Thompson Station area and served the entire West Harpeth community from his office in the front yard of his home on Columbia Pike. Dr. Greer grew up in South Harpeth, Tennessee, and was unusual in that he was practicing medicine before he received his diploma. He practiced in the Grassland community, living with the Moran family. He then moved over to Clovercroft and boarded with Sheddy Wilson, and was finally granted his medical degree from the University of Tennessee in Memphis. He took his state boards before he graduated in order to practice. Dr. Greer practiced until his death in 1939.

Three tollgates were on Columbia Pike between Spring Hill and Franklin, and as with all toll roads, it was a one-way toll. If one paid on the way into town, it was free on the way back home. At one time, Thomas B. Johnson owned all of Columbia Pike, until it was bought by the state around 1929. When that happened there was a big celebration, with speeches and plenty of food at the home of Dr. Hiram Laws. Dr. Laws was known for the fact he had a cannon on his front lawn, always facing north.

The West Harpeth community was at its peak between 1910 and 1925 before automobile travel reached the rural areas. With the coming of modern transportation, the community, as with so many others, changed, and businesses began to disappear. Some of the families who were the strength of West Harpeth were the Whitfield, Cunningham, Horton, Pitner, English, Rue, Jordan, Cowles, McLemore, Skidmore, Anderson, Greer, and Alexander families.

A number of West Harpeth residents who grew up together still live as neighbors in the community. Some have traveled worldwide and come back to Williamson County. They value their friendships and, like neighbors all over, care for each other and help in times of need. The buildings, like the West Harpeth granary, are in disrepair, but the people are as strong as they were seventy or eighty years ago when West Harpeth was more active.

Resources

The following individuals gave graciously of their time and historical information on the various communities. Louise Lynch and Virginia Bowman contributed in some manner to each of the forty-four articles.

Allisona
Mary Rigsby
Terry White
Della Covington Corlette
Zelma White
Bill Ogilvie

Arno
Red Jordan
Elder Milton Lillard
Harry Lillard
Alice Pollard
Louise Williams

Arrington
Hill Paschall
Evelyn Paschall
Sue P. Johnson

Ash Grove
Helen Cook Potts
William Potts
Charlene Ring
Margaret Sawyer
Jere Sawyer

Beechville
Sally Rodes Lee

Bending Chestnut
Gilbert Fox
T. C. Fox
Joe Burns
Harold Meacham
Harding Meacham

Berry Chapel
Nova McKay
Lula Fain Major

Bethesda
Leo Bond
Cleo Grigsby

Bingham
Hazel Blankenship
Richard Warwick
Barry Bingham
Sue Owen

Boston
Mary Trim Anderson
Mary Frances Marlin
Elmer Peach
Ruby Peach
Gladys House

Brentwood
T. Vance Little

Burwood
Judy G. Hayes
Abe Church
Polly Duncan
Farris Huff
Ken Huff
Katherine Cotton
Ollie Jo Sparkman
Louise Dedman
Leonard Grigsby

Callie
James William Hood

Clovercroft
Christine Wilson
Joe D. Wilson
Corrine Jones
Mary Herbert
Henry Mayberry

College Grove
J. Powell Covington
Jonnie Demonbreun
Mary Lizzie Manier

Craigfield
Leechie Barnhill
Gilbert Sullivan
L. D. Parham

Cross Keys
Carrie Trice
Herbert McCall
Mildred McCall
Josephine Trice Williams
Colonel Hensley Williams
James Trice
W. T. Skinner

Duplex
James Thompson
Rebecca Thompson
Brenda Rader Thompson
Ruth Thompson
Martha Lee

Fairview
C. C. Daugherty
Tom Taylor
Ione Sullivan
Virginia Fitzgerald
Annie Lee Hall
Earl Lampley
Martha Hall
T. Vance Little
Gilbert Sullivan
Luda Spicer Fisher

Flagpole
Sue Nell Green
Oscar Green

Flat Creek
Ennis Wallace Sr.
Allean Wallace

Forest Home
Mary Lynch
Leighla Carrol
Mary Roberts
Viola Roberts
Walter Roberts

Franklin
Judge John H. Henderson
Peggy Henderson Gentry
T. Vance Little

Grassland
Sally Rodes Lee
Harold Yeargin
Lula Fain Major

Greenbrier
Ethel Thompson
Billie Hay
Tom Fox

Harpeth
Walter Anderson
Tom Stoddard

Kingfield
Vera King
Walter King
Homa King

Kirkland
J. Powell Covington

Leiper's Fork
Mary Trim Anderson
Louise Green
T. Vance Little
Elna Sweeney Mangrum

Liberty
T. Vance Little

Liberty Hill
Luda Spicer Fisher
Gilbert Sullivan
Earl Lampley

Millview
Mary Kate Zimmerman
Charlie Fox Jr.
Evelyn Vaden

Mudsink
Elder Milton Lillard
Geneva Lillard
Ellis Lynch
Jim Lynch

New Hope
Gilbert Sullivan
Albert Luther Daugherty
Frances Daugherty

Nolensville
Newt McCord

Peytonsville
May Ellen Glenn
Tommy Glenn
Bill Ormes
John Glenn
Rebecca Meek

Riggs Crossroads
Carolyn Savage
Ann Johnson
John Gaultney
Elizabethine Mullette Gaultney

Rudderville
Abe Hatcher
Jackie Hatcher
Howard Smithson
Doris Smithson
Alice Pollard
Louise Williams

Southall
W. C. Yates
Katherine Yates
Louise Scivally
Robert Schmidt

Thompson Station
Katherine Cotton
Delores Kestner
Elva Darby

Trinity
Mary Herbert
Corrine Jones
Christine Wilson
Joe D. Wilson

Triune
Mildred Arnold

West Harpeth
John Jordan
Elizabeth Greer Pitner
Robert Pitner

173

Bibliography

Batey, Mrs. Marie Williams. "Mount Olivet Methodist Episcopal Church, South Nolensville, Tennessee." *Williamson County Historical Society Journal,* no. 10, 1979.

Betts, Ann. "Governor Newton Cannon Made His Mark." *The Tennessean,* Jan. 18, 1983.

———. "Leiper's Fork, Seems Combination of Old, New." *The Tennessean,* March 8, 1983.

———. "High Water Marks in Nolensville." *The Tennessean,* June 25, 1985.

Bingham, James Barry. *Descendants of James Bingham of County Down, Northern Ireland.* Baltimore: Gateway Press, Inc., 1980.

Bowman, Virginia McDaniel. *Historic Williamson County; Old Homes and Sites.* Nashville: Blue and Gray Press, 1971.

The Brentwood Journal, Sept. 25, 1985; Oct. 9, 1985; Nov. 6, 1985; Nov. 20, 1985.

Carlisle, Derry. "Who's Who in Williamson County." *The Review Appeal,* Jan. 20, 1972.

Cornwell, Ilene J. and T. Vance Little. "Leiper's Fork (Hillsboro)." *Williamson County Historical Society Journal,* no. 5, 1974.

Cotton, Katherine H. "A Look into the Past of Thompson Station." *Williamson County Historical Society Journal,* no. 10, 1979.

Covington, J. W. "Eastern Williamson County." *The Williamson County Historical Society Journal,* no. 10, 1979.

Crutchfield, James A. *The Harpeth River, A Biography.* Nashville: Blue and Gray Press, 1972.

———. *Williamson County, A Pictorial History.* Virginia Beach: The Donning Company, 1980.

Darby, Elva and William J. Darby. "Homestead Manor." *Williamson County Historical Society Journal,* no. 15, 1984.

Daugherty, Albert Luther. *An Autobiography of Albert Luther Daugherty,* 1980.

Dedman, Louise. "The Story of Burwood, Tennessee." *Williamson County Historical Society Journal,* no. 11, 1980.

Fleming Jr., Samuel M. *The Reminiscences of Newton Cannon, First Sergeant, C.S.A.* Jackson: McCowat-Mercer Press, Inc., 1963.

Gaultney, Elizabethine Mullette. "Riggs Crossroads." *Williamson County Historical Society Journal,* no. 15, 1984.

Gibbs, Mrs. Frances A. "The Town of Franklin, First Buyers of Town Lots." *Williamson County Historical Society Journal,* no. 13, 1982.

Jordan, John L. "History of Triune."

Little, T. Vance. "Brentwood, A Rich Heritage." *Williamson County Historical Society Journal,* no. 16, 1985.

———. "Dr William J. McMurray." *Williamson County Historical Society Journal,* no. 8, 1977.

———. *Historic Brentwood.* Brentwood: JM Publications, 1985.

———. "The Liberty Community." *Williamson County Historical Society Journal,* no. 10, 1979.

Lynch, Louise Gillespie. *Miscellaneous Records of Williamson County,* vols. II, III, and IV.

———. *Our Valiant Men.* Franklin, 1976.

———. "Mount Zion Methodist Episcopal Church." *Williamson County Historical Society Journal,* no. 2, 1971.

Major, Lula Fain. "Memories of Sunnyside School." *Williamson County Historical Society Journal,* no. 2, 1971.

———. "Garner McConnico." *Williamson County Historical Society Journal,* no. 8, 1976.

Marshall, Park. Articles from the *Williamson County News,* 1910 to 1920.

Mitchell, Enoch L. "Letters of a Confederate Surgeon in the Army of Tennessee to His Wife." *Tennessee Historical Quarterly,* vol. IV, Dec. 1945, and vol. V, March 1946.

Plummer, Eilene M. and Ilene J. Cornwall. "Fernvale Resort and Caney Fork Furnace." *Williamson County Historical Society Journal,* no. 4, 1973.

The Review-Appeal. Oct. 1963; 1974; July 1, 1976.

Trickey, Katherine Shelburne. "John Bell Also Ran." *Williamson County Historical Society Journal,* no. 15, 1984.

Webb, William S. "Articles on Williamson County Communities." *The Review-Appeal,* 1938 and 1939.

Williamson Churches. *The Williamson Leader.* One of a Series: April 21, 1974; June 2, 1974; June 16, 1974; Aug. 11, 1974; Oct. 13, 1974; Dec. 15, 1974; Jan. 19, 1975; Feb. 9, 1975; May 11, 1975; Aug. 3, 1975; Aug. 31, 1975; Aug. 17, 1975; Feb. 17, 1979.

Womack, Steve. "Arno's Wesley Chapel Methodist Church, 1834-1984." *Williamson County Historical Society Journal,* no. 16, 1985.

Index

Photo page numbers are in bold type.

175

176

177

178

180